SOME SIGHTS YOU'LL *NEVER* SEE FROM A TOUR BUS

Wild blackberry brambles ambling along a Burgundian roadside. . . . The lush—and still largely uninhabited—countryside that inspired Paul Cézanne. . . . A charming *boulangerie* where you can toast the day with the same *vin ordinaire* favored by Henry IV. . . . A scenic stop-off where you can buy *foie gras* at a backroad farmstand.

The rich sights, sounds, and flavors of France attract thousands of tourists each year. But some of the most unforgettable destinations of all are located on France's less-traveled byways. *Bicycle Tours of France* is your step-by-step guide off the beaten track . . . to unexpected places where real adventure begins! Places like:

- The Provençal village where shepherds use bicycles to herd their sheep
- The Cézanne country loop—dotted with historic châteaux and Roman ruins
- PLUS—Pedaling tips and complete directions to dozens of three-star restaurants and cozy wayside inns

GAY and KATHLYN HENDRICKS are psychologists who practice and teach in Colorado. They are also avid travelers who have toured all over the world on their bikes.

BICYCLE
TOURS
— OF —
FRANCE

GAY & KATHLYN HENDRICKS

BICYCLE TOURS
—— OF ——
FRANCE

℗

A PLUME BOOK

PLUME

Published by the Penguin Group
Penguin Books USA Inc., 375 Hudson Street, New York, New York 10014, U.S.A.
Penguin Books Ltd, 27 Wrights Lane, London W8 5TZ, England
Penguin Books Australia Ltd, Ringwood, Victoria, Australia
Penguin Books Canada Ltd, 10 Alcorn Avenue, Toronto, Ontario, Canada M4V 3B2
Penguin Books (N.Z.) Ltd, 182–190 Wairau Road, Auckland 10, New Zealand

Penguin Books Ltd, Registered Offices:
Harmondsworth, Middlesex, England

First published by Plume,
an imprint of New American Library,
a division of Penguin Books USA Inc.

First Printing, April, 1992
1   3   5   7   9   10   8   6   4   2

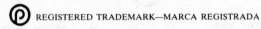 REGISTERED TRADEMARK—MARCA REGISTRADA

LIBRARY OF CONGRESS CATALOGING IN PUBLICATION DATA:

Hendricks, Gay.
   Bicycle tours of France / Gay and Kathlyn Hendricks.
   p.   cm.
   ISBN 0-452-26773-0
   1. Bicycle touring—France—Guide-books.   2. France—Description
and travel—1975—Guide-books.   I. Hendricks, Kathlyn.
II. Title.
GV1046.F8H46   1992
796.6'4'0944—dc20   91–34322
                                                                CIP

Printed in the United States of America
Set in Times Roman

Designed by Steven N. Stathakis

WARNING!

Bicycling is a strenuous sport. Before embarking on these tours, it is advisable to check with your physician to make sure you are in sound enough health to cope with the rigors of several hours of physically demanding exercise a day.

CONTENTS

PART TWO: THE FIVE TOURS

NOTE

The authors have accepted no complimentary rooms, meals, or gifts throughout any of the tours described in this book. Similarly, we have not traveled with or on any gift equipment of any kind. Therefore, you can be assured that our recommendations are based solely on personal opinion. Likewise, any opinions we express are solely our responsibility.

PART ONE

WHAT YOU NEED TO KNOW ABOUT TOURING IN FRANCE

INTRODUCTION:

WHY GO BICYCLE

TOURING IN FRANCE?

I was not yet sixteen when I understood a great deal, from having ridden bicycles for so long, about style, speed, grace, purpose, value, form, integrity, health, humor, music, breathing, and finally and perhaps best of all, the relationship between the beginning and the end.
—WILLIAM SAROYAN, from *The Bicycle Rider in Beverly Hills*

WOULD YOU ENJOY A DAY LIKE THE ONE WE SPENT NOT long ago?

We awoke in a small country inn to the smell of rich French roast coffee and croissants fresh from the oven. Our inn overlooked rolling farmland, with the vineyards of the Côte-d'Or in the distant morning mist. Our room was a tasteful combination of feather-comforter antiquity and up-to-date conveniences. After a stint in the largest bathtub we had ever occupied, it was down to breakfast in the tiny dining room. Huge steaming mugs of coffee appeared, along with a little jug of fresh cream from the farmer next door. A basket of croissants followed, still hot from the oven.

Soon Madame came out from the kitchen to inquire, in beautifully accented English, whether we had enjoyed our breakfast. With two croissants apiece now history and several cups—bowls, really—of the rich coffee fueling our blood-streams, all we could do was smile. We complimented her cuisine, her exquisite taste in bedroom furnishings, and especially, her way with a coffeepot. We paid our bill and were soon on our way.

Outside the September sun was beginning to shine in earnest, having burned off the early morning haze. We saddled up our bikes and were soon pedaling down a narrow road toward the slopes of the Côte-d'Or. The grape harvest was in full swing, and all morning long we passed groups of men and women bent over the precious grapes. They stopped to wave as we passed, and occasionally tossed us a small bunch of grapes. For the next three hours, we wound through some of the real estate most sacred to wine fanciers: Gevrey-Chambertin, Pouilly and Fuissé. In these precious vineyards, every inch of soil is conserved and carefully tended: Workers literally wipe their feet before leaving the fields in order to keep the soil where it belongs. These towns are perfectly suited to bike travel. On a bicycle you can wend your way through the tiny lanes and back roads of the region—and never have to deal with car traffic unless you want to.

After twenty miles or so of cruising up and down the gentle slopes of the region, we were ready for a break. The croissants had worn off, but since we knew a major feast awaited us at dinner, a light lunch was called for. At a tiny *boulangerie* we selected a round of crusty bread and two custard tarts. A bottle of water and a slab of local cheese completed the picnic, which we spread under the shade of an ancient tree in the backyard of a château. After lunch, we curled up by our bikes for a short nap.

The afternoon's ride took us away from the vineyards into the sparsely populated back country. We rolled down deserted country roads flanked by wild blackberry bushes. The blackberries were in the peak of ripeness that week, and every now and then we would pause for a sweet handful. By five o'clock our bodies had that kind of relaxed exhaustion that seems especially to accompany biking. With the help of our map, we located our inn, a large château that had been turned into a hotel some twenty-five years before. It had stone walls and massive timber beams and was set on a hillside overlooking a quiet valley. After a bath and a rest, we dressed for dinner at our first world-class restaurant on this trip. Highlights of that meal were: a skewer with two tiny squares of broiled salmon and two squares of *foie gras* on it; a warm slice of duck breast smothered in morels—a classic example of Burgundian cooking, rich meat simmered in an even richer dark gravy with a strong undercurrent of red wine; and dessert, a simple affair of eight or ten tiny fresh-baked canapés and cookies, arranged among flowers on a gleaming silver tray. Coffee and the chef's own chocolates completed the evening. We were grateful for the five-plus hours of cycling earlier in the day. But far from feeling stuffed, we felt replenished and ready for the next day in the saddle.

A few seconds after we pulled the down comforter up around our chins that night, we were sound asleep and stayed that way until the smell of coffee awakened us for another day's adventure.

GENERAL INFORMATION

ON BICYCLE TOURING

IN FRANCE

WHAT KIND OF TOUR SHOULD YOU TAKE? GOING SOLO VS. AN ORGANIZED TOUR

THERE IS ONLY ONE CHOICE YOU NEED TO MAKE TO GET started—whether to go solo or to take an organized tour. Your choice will determine other factors, such as whether you will be renting a bike or taking your own. Both styles have advantages and disadvantages. For the first time out, it is easiest to join an organized tour. This is how we did it the first time, and looking back, we are grateful to have done so.

The greatest advantage of an organized tour is that someone else handles the logistical details. Join a tour and you will be handed a marked map in the morning and the key to your room at night. Your restaurants are chosen for you, the best little roads are pointed out, and your bike is kept in good working order. Above all, a sagwagon follows with your luggage and, should you need to, you can hitch a ride, too. These details can be frustrating when added to a full day of bicycling.

Another advantage of an organized tour is that you have a ready-made social group. There will usually be no shortage of dinner table companions or fellow wine connoisseurs with whom to visit the local vineyards. The downside to such a prefab social configuration, though, is that you could be stuck with a bunch of people you don't like. Usually there is plenty of space, even on an organized tour, to spread out and do your own trip, but the evenings will often be spent in marathon dining.

For many, cost is a major consideration of an organized tour. Plan on spending around $200 per person for each day. Our first tour was an eight-day affair that cost $1695. For both of us, then, the cost was $3400 for an eight-day trip. Of course, this price did not include airfare or a few days in Paris on either end. If you travel as a twosome, you are consuming one night's lodging, two continental breakfasts, and two dinners. Lunch will almost always be on your own, although most tours feature a picnic or two at the company's expense. On our first organized tour we noted the cost of the rooms, which were always displayed on the door. Seldom were they over $50; seldom were the dinners more than $50 per person. So, even if you throw in $10 apiece for croissants and coffee, we were paying $200 to $250 a day for maps, the sagwagon, and a guide.

The first time out, you may find it worth it to pay the premium. But on future trips we bet you will go solo. Going solo, or with a few close friends, has tremendous advantages. You are free to make your own choices. With a little advance planning, a good map, and the *Guide Michelin*, you can do your own trip. With that extra $200 a day in your pocket, go wild with a couple of dinners at a three-star restaurant.

Let's look into some of the details of going solo. One word that sums up the difference is *weight*. You will definitely have to carry about ten pounds of your clothing, toiletries, and other essentials in your panniers. This fact encourages you to be a light traveler, a virtue worth cultivating. Ten extra pounds makes your bike pedal harder and handle a little differently. Neither of these considerations is earthshaking, in our experience, but you should build it into your plans. Put ten pounds extra on your bike when you are getting in shape for the trip. It is not wise to wait until you get there to find out how a loaded bike handles. If you decide you want to camp out throughout your tour, you should double the weight estimate to twenty-plus pounds.

Another attractive option is to take your own bikes and rent a car to haul them from place to place. Renting a car in France is no problem, but it is expensive. Plan on double what you might pay in the U.S. The tax on car rentals was 28 percent last time we did it, and you have a stiff insurance cost plus high fuel bills to consider. With gas going for the equivalent of $4 to $5 a gallon, you will appreciate the tiny cars they drive over there. Nevertheless, renting a car makes life easier and certainly increases your mobility. You won't be at the mercy of the train schedule, and you can get to many places you might skip without a car. On one of our recent tours we rented a car and made one town our base in each area we wanted to tour. Then we would do day-loops, returning to home base at night, or we would drive the car to a new area and ride from there each day.

This book is written with the adventurous but comfort-loving bicycle tourer in mind. You travel light, you stay at inns, and you only carry a modest amount of weight on your bike. (Readers who want to find out about camping in Europe can find a great deal of useful information on that subject in "budget" books such as the *Let's Go* guides.)

After many different kinds of trips, our unhesitating recommendation is to go solo or with close friends, take your own bikes, tour specific regions (such as the five great trips described in this book), and get from region to region by train. An evening or two of advance planning, all of which you can do with the information included here, will yield the easy assurance that you will always have a bed waiting for you at the end of the day.

WHAT KIND OF BIKE IS BEST? HOW DO YOU GET IT THERE?

Our opinion: *Take your own bike, preferably a mountain bike.* Here's why. Renting a bicycle sounds like a good idea, but in fact, it is usually a disaster. For example, once, we attempted to rent bikes in a large Scottish city. According to the travel guide we were using (never again!), there were oodles of bike shops, all bursting with rental bikes. After going to three bike shops, we found one that rented bikes and were shown to a dim room. The owner invited us to pick out the ones we wanted. After a half-hour of searching, we found two which only needed minor repairs (most of the others were suitable only for scrap metal). We told the owner the repairs that needed to be done, he nodded gravely, and returned in a few minutes with a pair of pliers and a couple of terminally greasy wrenches. He handed these to us and left for the day, telling us to stuff the tools under the doormat when we were finished. On another occasion, we wanted to rent bikes in Chengdu, China, a city of several million people and at least a million bikes. We were shown to an underground garage with bicycles as far as the eye could see. But we had to sort through over thirty bikes to find ones on which the brakes worked.

Enough said. With luck, however, you might find a good bike shop with well-kept rentals.

HOW TO RENT A BIKE

If you are in Europe without a bike and want to rent one for short day trips, you will find a wide variety of rental places in major cities. Many train stations rent sturdy bikes in various states of repair. In Paris, Le Cyclobus, in the Bois de Bologne near the Hippodrôme, has decent bikes by the hour or by the day. Another option is Paris Velo (tel. 43–37–59–22), which has better bikes at a higher price; you can rent them for as long as you like.

A better idea is to ask the concierge where you're staying for a recommendation; concierges often have up-to-date information on which places rent the most reliable bikes nearby.

Riding a bike in Paris, though, is only for the adventurous or the deranged. The traffic is heavy, and while the French are most respectful of cyclists in the country, they are quite impatient in the city. Best to take a train to the hinterlands and get your bike there; ride the Metro around Paris. A typical price for a day's rental, both in and outside of Paris, is 33 francs, a little over $5. This price drops to a little over $4 a day if you keep the bike three to ten days, and to about $3 a day if you keep the bike eleven days or more.

TAKING YOUR OWN BIKE

Taking your own bike is not as hard as it sounds, and you will know what you are getting. We recommend mountain bikes. Yes, they are a little heavier than touring bikes, but they ride more comfortably. Many of the choice roads you will want to ride can be rough. And European towns, even larger ones, have cobblestone streets. These are pretty to look at but brain-rattlingly difficult on a thin-tired bike. With your fat-tired mountain bike, you will bump pleasantly over cobblestones and charge down primitive country lanes. Even dirt roads will be an option. If you keep your mountain bike tires properly inflated, flats will be very rare. Not so on a thin-tired bike, where by our rough count over the years, we averaged about one flat a week. Since switching to mountain bikes some years ago, we have had only three flats all told. In fact, on our roughest trip, a two-week journey through Tibet, we never had a single flat. If you already have a sturdy touring bike, by all means take it. But if you are just getting started, at least consider mountain bikes.

Airline regulations vary with regard to fare and how you take your bike. Many airlines take bikes free, but check in advance so you won't be surprised. Some airlines do not make you pack your bike in a box, while others are adamant on the subject. Putting a bike in a box is not difficult, but requires a visit to a bike shop to pick up the carton. It also requires a few minutes of work with simple tools. You need to remove the pedals, turn the handlebars sideways, and usually, remove at least the front wheel. The airport is not the place to do this operation for the first time. With mountain bikes, turning the handlebars may be more difficult, requiring loosening the brake cables. A few minutes at a bike shop is usually sufficient to learn how to do this on your particular bike.

Here is a suggestion. Show up at the airport, with your bike and the tools you will need. Bring a carton, but leave it over in the corner. Act as though you expect the airline to take your bike without putting it in a box. Sometimes they will and sometimes they won't. Sometimes they will give you the same heavy plastic used to wrap skis. This is better than a box, because putting the bike out of sight in a box increases your chances of damage. The guys who handle baggage are more likely to be rough with a bike they cannot see than one they can. Most people, even baggage handlers, have some positive childhood associations with bikes and will not knowingly do violence to them. You should know, though, that in our experience the most dangerous part of your bike's journey is while it is in the hands of the airline. This is another argument for taking mountain bikes; they are much more rugged than their lighter cousins. Regardless, you need to be prepared to do some adjusting and even repairing when you arrive at your destination. On a couple of occasions, we have had to make a trip to a local bicycle shop on arrival, to repair some damage done to a bike on the flight over. It takes a little time, but we have yet to be in a country where there was not someone with a wrench who could do the repair.

BUYING A BIKE IN EUROPE

Another option is to buy a bicycle when you get to Europe. Many people think they can get a good bargain that way. Forget it. This might have been true in the past, but no longer. Some people think they can get a higher quality machine in Europe than they can in the U.S. Again, forget it. With a couple of rare and expensive exceptions, you will find better quality in a good American or Japanese bike than you will in a European model. We ride Klein, Trek, and Stumpjumper machines, and we have yet to see anything in Europe we would trade them for.

USING TRAINS ON A BIKE TOUR

Bikes and trains are a perfect combination. We are *train-worshippers*. We find trains to be both exciting and restful ways to travel. All trains will let you take your bike, though the exact procedure has some variations. Europeans, particularly the French and the Italians, are very respectful of bikes. Your bike will be well treated, and theft is rare, though of course you need to bring a chain and lock.

In France, the charge is usually the equivalent of a few dollars. Your bike may in certain circumstances go on a different train than you, especially if you are going on an express train. Don't worry—we haven't heard of any cases where the bikes disappeared. But sometimes there can be a delay of a few hours or a day until your bike arrives. The rail company guarantees that it will arrive within seventy-two hours. Usually the station will hold it free for a day, but if you leave it longer you can expect a charge. Bikes are such an integral part of life in Europe that the policies are well worked out, even though they vary slightly from place to place. If you encounter an obstacle, such as a train official who tells you that under no circumstances can you take your bike to wherever you are going, persist. Go higher up. A way can usually be found. Once we stood in line behind an English biker who wanted to go from Tours to Nice, in the south of France.

"Utterly impossible," said the clerk, who was not having a good day. "Bikes not allowed on this train." Much argument ensued. Finally the clerk went on break, and was replaced by another fellow. "Absolutely. No problem, monsieur." Within minutes the Englishman was on his way to Nice, bike and all.

Here is the general step-by-step procedure to follow in French railway stations. First, buy your ticket. With ticket in hand, go to the baggage counter and choose the train. Try to find one that takes accompanying baggage (since this will allow you to go on the same train as your bike). Next, register your bike by filling out a form (you should get a receipt); remove all the easily stolen items like pump, water bottle, and handlebar packs, and hand over your bike. It is possible to buy insurance for your bike for 10 francs per 1000 francs of the bike's value. (For a $500 bike, your insurance will cost you about $5.) We have never bought it, but it certainly is reasonable if you want it. Some railway stations also have a cardboard envelope called a *carton de velo* that fits around your bike. These cost about 10 francs.

Next, if you are taking one of the bullet trains (TGV), you will need to make your own reservation. Otherwise, it's not necessary to reserve. Get on the right train, and pick up your bike on the other end by handing over your receipt. Sometimes your bike, enshrouded in the mists of Gallic railway obscurity, will not arrive when you do, and you will need to come back a couple of times to find it. If you are picking up your bike at an out-of-the-way station, don't be upset if there's nobody home between 12 and 2 P.M. This is the sacred hour when the French worship lunch.

Does all this sound complicated? It's not, really, and after a few times it will make perfect sense.

WHEN TO GO: WEATHER, FELLOW TRAVELERS, AND SUCH

You may be wondering what happens if it rains during your tour. The answer: You stay inside that day, or you get wet.

In our experience, it doesn't happen often. We can only remember a few days of being absolutely stopped by the
weather. Part of the trick is good clothing; part of it is good
planning. A lot of it is good luck.

Gore-Tex is one of the greatest friends of the bicycle
tourer. We have Gore-Tex jackets in two weights, along with
riding pants made of the same material. These items have
been worth their weight in gold during many trips. We have
given up rain capes in favor of the Gore-Tex jacket-pants
combination. Gore-Tex is expensive, but will make up for its
cost in convenience and long-term use. The material is also
useful in dealing with wind, which is an even bigger challenge
than rain.

Wind can be heartbreaking as well as heart-pounding. On
a recent tour we climbed 10 miles steadily uphill to a mountain pass, dreaming of the ride down from the top. Alas, when
we got to the top we found a headwind blowing at gale force.
We rode downhill in *first* gear, straining all the way against
the wind at about 1 mile an hour. It was psychologically dis-
couraging as well as physically exhausting. On the flip side,
we have enjoyed some inspiring tailwinds. There is nothing
like the exhilaration of flying down a road at 25 miles an hour
with only the barest effort.

Rain and wind can be obstacles at times, but neither
needs to be monitored like heat. Unless you plan ahead and
drink in advance, you can get in serious trouble by dehydrat-
ing yourself. By the time you get thirsty you may have already
gone past the critical point. We have seen many a cyclist with
a flushed face, a headache, and quivering legs, all from ignor-
ing the body's need for water. Plan ahead. Drink a few
extra glasses of water in the morning, and keep drinking as
you go along, even if you are not thirsty. If you don't trust
the local water, you will find noncarbonated bottled water
everywhere.

There are some places and times of the year when it is
not wise to ride in the middle of the day. As the summer goes
on, southern parts of Europe, especially Italy and Spain, can
get brutally hot. But a hot snap can happen anywhere, and
you will simply have to monitor the weather. Get on the road

early, and take a siesta from noon to five or so. The depleted feeling you can get from too much sun and heat can be especially enervating on a bike, as the wind on your body will often make you feel cooler than you are.

A glance at the following chart may help you decide when to go.

AVERAGE FAHRENHEIT TEMPERATURE AND PRECIPITATION IN INCHES FOR THREE CITIES IN FRANCE

	MAY	JUNE	JULY	AUGUST	SEPTEMBER
Paris	55°F.	62	65	64	58
	1.9"	2.2	2.0	1.9	1.9
Bordeaux	60	65	69	69	65
	2.8	2.8	2.0	1.9	2.3
Nice	62	69	73	73	69
	2.8	1.0	0.7	1.3	3.0

Remember that charts can never be more than a general help. One reason is that the weather is not controlled by the people who make the charts. Our two tours with the best weather were in May and September in the environs of Bordeaux. On these tours we did not have one day of rain, in spite of what the chart says. Come to think of it, we didn't have an hour of rain that occurred when we wanted to be riding. Also remember that other factors play a role. In spite of the chart's favorable opinion of August, it is the month when all Parisians who can do so traditionally empty the capital and head for the countryside. They will want to stay at the same inns and eat at the same restaurants you do. If you want to go to France in August, it is imperative that you make plenty of advance reservations. If you don't like crowds, May and

September are perfect months to travel. Service is better, the roads are quieter, and the weather can often be wonderful.

On our last tour through the French wine country we had perfect weather—not a day of riding was missed because of rain. Yet the following week a colleague of ours went touring down south in Provence, and he was inundated nine out of twelve days in an area which is usually dry. So there are no guarantees, and the chart can often be maddeningly wrong. Our suggestion: Pick a time when you can do it—and do it. Do your planning, and don't worry about the weather. Chances are you will not be inconvenienced by the weather more than a couple of times. If you are, there are worse things in life than a stroll around a French town on a rainy afternoon or a long day under the covers.

WHAT TO TAKE AND WHAT NOT TO TAKE: CLOTHING AND OTHER NECESSITIES OF THE ROAD

The most practical and efficient way to pack is to take no more than your panniers can carry. If you get a good pair of panniers, they will serve as your carry-on luggage on the airplane. Pannier design is changing rapidly, and whatever advice we might give you would probably be obsolete by the time you read this. Visit a good bike shop, and tell them what you are looking for: high quality panniers that attach and detach easily, have plenty of room, and are easy to pack and repack. They should be as waterproof as you can afford and made of an easily cleaned, machine-washable material.

Here is what we took on a recent tour through the wine country. It is a fairly good representation of what is needed on a one-week tour. On this particular tour we were going to be dining at several very fancy restaurants, so we needed clothing that would not make us look out of place.

RIDING CLOTHES AND EQUIPMENT

helmet, gloves
Gore-Tex jacket and pants
2 pairs of riding shorts (the kind with reinforced seats)
3 cotton T-shirts
3 pairs of socks
1 pair of silk thermal underwear
1 pair of running shoes (special bike touring shoes are available which
     are also comfortable enough for walking, but we have found
     that good running shoes work just as well)

CASUAL AND FANCY WEAR·

1 pair of jeans
1 pair of casual slacks
1 light wool sweater
1 pair of dress shoes
underwear
(for Kathlyn) 2 silk evening outfits—slacks, top, and matching jacket
2 pairs of dress socks/stockings
(for Gay) 1 indestructible wool sport coat
2 shirts
1 tie

MISCELLANEOUS

toiletries, carefully chosen and packed in a small kit (take a roll of
     your favorite brand of toilet paper, as the French have quaint
     ideas on this subject)
small first-aid kit, including Band-Aids, antiseptic cream, aspirin,
     tweezers, scissors, moleskin
bathing suits
sunglasses
sunscreen and lip cream (absolutely essential)
camera
tool kit, chain lubricant, 2 spare tubes (your water bottle and pump
     fit on your bike, so we are not counting those)

Total weight apiece: slightly under 10 pounds

You may want to invest in a handlebar pack or "fanny" pack. It is nice to be able to get at frequently used items (like lip cream and camera) without opening your panniers. If you buy the kind that straps around your waist you can also use it as a day-pack when you are on foot.

CHOOSING WHERE TO STAY

Fortunately for the cyclist, France is chock-full of fine accommodations. The range is limited only by your pocketbook. Unlike England, France does not have an abundance of lower-priced lodgings that would be called bed and breakfasts elsewhere. In the countryside you will find country inns, small hotels, and châteaux. We have preferred to seek out quiet, small inns on our journeys, so that is what we recommend in this book. Every area of France we have toured has had tourist information offices with up-to-date listings of the available accommodations. We have visited these offices many, many times, and have always been impressed with their efficiency. If you avoid touring in the height of summer (July and August), you may not need to make any reservations. We have seldom made reservations on our tours, simply because we like to have a bit more flexibility. However, we realize there are plenty of people who are uncomfortable with not knowing where they will sleep that night. If you choose not to make reservations, we have good news for you. We have not yet been forced to sleep out in the rain. The only trouble we ever had with finding a place to stay was one night in 1980 in the heart of Paris. It took until 2 A.M., wandering around various neighborhoods, until we found a little hotel.

Although we have recommended many fine hotels in this book, we encourage adventurous cyclists to be their own *Guide Michelin*. We found most of these hotels by word-of-mouth or in the *Guide* by accident. If you keep an open mind and an optimistic attitude, you will likely find wonders that have hitherto been hidden.

WHAT AND HOW TO EAT: RESTAURANTS, *BOULANGERIES*, *BRASSERIES*, GROCERY SHOPPING

Food and athletic performance is a subject of much controversy. To steer clear of it, we will simply tell you how we have found it best to eat on a tour. You can try our approach; feel free to modify it, or change it altogether to suit your particular metabolism. First, we do not like to load up with a big breakfast in the morning. Coffee and a couple of croissants are perfect. As it happens, this traditional French breakfast is available everywhere, though sometimes it is transformed into rolls, butter, and jelly. Complex carbohydrates are good energy food and sit lightly in the stomach. This latter consideration is an important one for us; we do not like to pedal with a full sensation in the belly. We prefer to breakfast lightly and then eat frequent light snacks as the day proceeds. This habit has enabled us to explore the treasures of many French grocery stores, which we love because of their unusual and exotic fare. Recently, for amusement, we counted the varieties of yogurt in one supermarket in central France. There were twenty-nine, including samples from Bulgaria, Greece, and Switzerland. As yogurt fanciers, we can get as excited about an obscure Bulgarian yogurt as some might over finding a rare wine. You can find just about anything you might crave in French grocery stores, and plenty of things you might not have imagined. In France you can even get mustard and mayonnaise in tubes, a great idea that we hope catches on in the U.S. If we are going to have a big protein-rich meal, we do it at night, after the main exercise of the day is over.

Finding great cycling food is not difficult in France; resisting it is difficult. Even towns of modest size will have a wonderful bakery, full of luscious tarts, cakes, and cookies. For this reason, we urge you not to bring your diet consciousness to France with you. Even if you've been a macrocosmic vegetarian for years, try something different for a change.

Take a break from your eating habits and get into theirs for a week or two. You may not want to eat their way for the rest of your life, but enjoy it while you are there. After a couple of weeks of triple-cream cheese, *foie gras,* and butter-drenched *escargot,* you may be grateful to get back to your bean sprouts and brown rice.

For those of you who are weight conscious, bike touring is a blessing. France can be a very broadening place in which to travel. But it is hard to gain much weight while you are pedaling five or six hours a day. Biking burns up 300–600 calories an hour (compared to approximately 80 calories an hour watching TV), so you can chow down with impunity. On one trip we each lost about five pounds, while on another we each gained two or three. It is interesting that even on a crosscountry bike trip of a couple of months, you will likely not gain or lose much weight. You will probably look leaner because of more muscle tissue, but the people we have talked to about their long-distance journeys say they stayed about the same weight.

The French table is a focal point (if not *the* focal point) of French life. More than one chef has been known to close his restaurant for the day because he did not find the right quality of ingredients when he went shopping that morning. According to one recent survey, Parisians spent 40 percent of their income on food. When going to France, then, it is wise to honor the French reverence for the art of cuisine. We grew up on dishes like tuna casserole, macaroni and cheese, and Swanson chicken pot pies, but we have learned to honor food more since spending time in France. We now take more care with our shopping and our preparing of food. We still prefer healthy, light fare, but we pay it more attention than we did before watching the French at table.

One of our most refreshing findings was that high prices do not always mean quality. Some incredibly expensive and famous dining establishments are simply tourist traps. Many are wonderful, of course, and we will tell you about some of the finest as we describe the tours. But a truly special thing about France is that you can discover an unheralded country inn or neighborhood restaurant that serves the transcendent

soup or the unforgettable dessert. These are the special moments you will always remember, because they will be free of
pomp, circumstance, and hype. You will simply be treated to
the cooking of someone who adores food. Our best meals in
France have always been at out-of-the-way restaurants.

If you are inclined to the conservative in matters of food,
here is your chance to stretch. Do something we have done:
Order a dish on the menu that you cannot translate. In other
words, order it and be surprised at what you get. What, you
may exclaim, if I get snails or some sort of obscure organ?
Eat it!—you may be surprised. We personally never thought
we would enjoy sweetbreads or truffles or snails before going
to France. Now we think about them a lot between trips.

WINE, BEER, WATER, AND LIQUOR

Just as it is hard to find a bad meal in France, it is very hard
to get bad wine in a French restaurant. We are not big wine
drinkers, so many of our experiences come from ordering a
demi-pichet, or half-carafe, of a house wine. We have usually
been delighted with the quality of the wine ordered in this
manner. Another thing we have frequently done is tell the
sommelier, if it's a fancy restaurant (or our waiter, if it's a
more modest one), exactly the taste and price we are looking
for. We may ask, "Can you recommend a semidry white for
under seventy francs [$10–11]?" On almost every occasion we
have found that the service staff is genuinely interested in
helping you choose a good wine. Encounters with the famous
surly snarl of the French have been blessedly few and far
between.

To start a meal, the French tend to drink lighter aperitifs
rather than heavier spirits such as whiskey or gin. Aperitifs
do not bomb the palate into submission; rather, they seem to
heighten taste and appetite. One common tasty aperitif is the
kir royale, which is a fruit liqueur such as raspberry mixed
with champagne. France, while not widely known for beer,
nevertheless has several good ones. We have tried Fischer,
Kronenbourg, and several others whose names we've forgot-
ten, all of which are superior to any American beer and in

the same league as their more famous German cousins. If you want a draft, ask for *un pression*; a short draft is *un demi-pression*.

Bottled water is available everywhere. The tap water in France is generally good, but we tend to order bottled. The famous ones are Evian (uncarbonated) and Perrier (carbonated), but there are many other delicious local brands.

MISCELLANEOUS MATTERS

THEFT

On a less pleasant subject, you do have to watch out for thieves in France, especially around Paris and Marseilles. Paris is justly notorious for its pickpockets and purse-snatchers, while many people in Marseilles and on the Riviera make their sole living from thievery. Other provinces are much safer. Most of our tours are in places where theft is not common, but you should take precautions everywhere. Lock your bike, take your pump and pack with you at all times when you leave your bike, and keep a firm grip on your handbags. We always make a point, especially in Paris, of carrying our bags over the shoulder and under our arms, rather than swinging freely from our hands.

CUSTOMS

French customs, especially if you enter at airports, can be trying. On our last trip we arrived in the morning after an all-night flight from the U.S. We were stiff and grainy-eyed from a semisleepless night. There was one lone woman at the customs desk to stamp in over three hundred travelers! While there were a number of officials studiously watching her stamp our passports, she was the only one working. She took her time with it, so we spent our first couple of hours in France standing in line in a foul mood. We hope you have better luck, but our rule of thumb is that customs takes longer the further south and east you go in Europe.

Eventually you will get in, though, and you may bring with you two bottles of wine and one bottle of liquor. You may also bring two hundred cigarettes or fifty cigars. You can have two cameras, with ten rolls of film for each, and a movie camera or video camera with ten tapes or rolls of film. When you come back to the U.S., you can bring back $400 worth of goods without paying duty, provided you have been outside the U.S. for forty-eight hours or more. However, you can only do this once every thirty days. Items like perfume and wine and truffles can mount up quickly, so make sure you keep your receipts if you are trying to stay within the $400 allowance.

TELEPHONES

The French telephone system is a mix of modern and ancient. The modern system works with coins, usually accepting denominations of 50 centimes, 1 franc, and 5 francs. Make your transatlantic calls from the modern booths. The older apparatuses operate with little tokens called *jetons*, which you can buy at cafés, tobacconists, and the post office. Beware of the ease of making your calls from your hotel; they can put an outrageous surcharge on each call. Sometimes this can triple the cost of your call. The worst phone horror story we heard in France was of a man who did not hang up the phone properly after an overseas call, leaving the line open while he slept. The next day, on checking out, he received a phone bill for several thousand dollars.

To make calls to the U.S. and Canada from France, dial 19, wait for a tone, then dial 1, the area code, and the number. To make long distance calls from one part of France to another, dial 16, wait for the tone, then dial the number. French phone numbers have eight digits.

GETTING LAUNDRY DONE

Almost all hotels and inns will see to it that your laundry is done, and done well, but it tends to be two or three times the cost of doing it yourself. Laundries you find on the streets that do it for you will often charge less than the hotel, but make sure you pin them down on how long it will take. Once, some friends of ours had to delay their departure by several days because of a communication breakdown about when their clothes would be done. If you are having your Gore-Tex articles done by a laundry, make sure they wash it, not dry-clean it. Some cyclists we knew got their Gore-Tex back carefully dry-cleaned, and thus eaten alive by chemicals.

CLOSINGS AND HOLIDAYS

Think of it this way: Just about everything closes for lunch and on Sunday. Many things also close on Monday. To protect yourself, call first, because some restaurants have peculiar closings, such as for Wednesday lunch or Tuesday dinner. French holidays include Christmas and New Year's Day, May 1 (their Labor Day), Shrove Tuesday (the Tuesday before Ash Wednesday), Good Friday and Easter, Ascension Day (forty days after Easter), July 14 (Bastille Day), August 15 (Assumption Day), November 1 (All Saints' Day), and November 11 (Armistice Day).

GENERAL HINTS,
TIPS, AND STRATEGIES
FOR BICYCLE TOURING

IN THIS CHAPTER WE WILL COVER A NUMBER OF THOSE aspects of bike touring that you might otherwise have to learn the hard way. In fact, that's the way we learned many of these skills—by making a lot of mistakes. Perhaps you will be able to save yourself time, energy, and sore anatomy by trying out some of this hard-won wisdom.

SAFETY

The most important part of any tour is staying healthy and intact. Europe is probably the safest populated place on earth to ride your bike—and France is especially safe—but you still will need to keep an eye out for your well-being all the time. Where possible, stay off the heavily trafficked *N* roads (these designate the *Route National* highways maintained by the government). All our tours steer you toward *D* roads and their even smaller country cousins. There are times, however, especially when entering or leaving cities, when it is hard to avoid an *N* road or some other crowded thoroughfare, and you will need to exercise extra caution in these moments. For some reason we have never figured out, France has more trucks on the highway than any place we have seen. French truck drivers consider it an affront to their manhood to go less than 70 miles an hour, so look out for them. Except for the wine country during harvest time, you won't see many trucks on the roads we describe in our tours. On the back roads, bicyclists are given great respect and a wide berth by the typical driver. We rode the length of the Burgundy region at the peak of the grape harvest one year and saw only waves and salutes from the truck drivers. Out on the *N* roads, however, you are in their territory and cannot expect such courtesies.

We *always* wear **helmets**, even if we are just going around the block. We urge you to do so, too. You won't see a lot of helmets on French cyclists, so it may take some extra effort on your part to put it on every day. We are happy to choose safety over machismo. We have seen too many injuries that could have easily been prevented by simply strapping on a helmet. A friend's father, a vigorous man in the peak of health, nudged a curb a few blocks from his house and took a fall while going probably 2 miles an hour. He hit his head on the sidewalk and died from it instantly. Events like this have inspired us to buy the best helmet we could afford and to wear it wherever we go.

The same goes for **eye protection.** We always wear sunglasses, even on short rides. You never know when a stray bug is going to fly your way, so it pays to be prepared. Wraparound glasses or goggles are the way to go, because of increased protection against wind and glare. Wind is hard on eyes, because evolution has not provided for our rushing through space against the wind hours at a time. Glare is a major source of end-of-the-day headaches, so anything you can do to cut it down is to your advantage. Some of the new sunglasses are absolutely incredible—much better than anything that was available just a few years ago. We recently upgraded our old goggles to the new wraparound Oakley's and were amazed at the difference they made.

Mirrors have also come to be important to us. Gay wears the kind of rearview mirror that attaches to his glasses, while Kathlyn has the kind that attaches to the left side of the handlebars. Both of us swear by our choices. The great advantage of a rearview mirror is that you don't have to keep whipping your head around to see what's coming up behind you. This prevents stiff necks the next morning, as well as simply being more efficient. A glance in the mirror takes much less time than craning the neck around, and you run less danger of missteering your bike while looking back. We personally think rearview mirrors are real lifesavers, so we urge you to try them out.

Roadsigns in France sometimes take some ingenuity to translate. In general, round signs give orders, rectangular signs give information, and triangular signs give warnings. Here are some of the most common, along with explanations.

red ring around bicycle	No bikes allowed
white bar across red background	Wrong way—No entry
white bike on blue background	Pedal bikes only
black hump/red border	Bumpy road
black train/red border	Rail crossing, no barrier
black gate/red border	Rail crossing, barrier
exclamation point	Danger
car going into water	Bank, dock
small letter **i**	Tourist information

DAILY MAINTENANCE

If you will pay your bike just a few minutes of attention each day, it will reward you with hours of service. Neglect those few minutes, however, and look out. Many of the safety problems people have on bike rides come from not noticing little things that need a tiny bit of adjusting. An improperly tightened quick release or a worn brake cable can make a very large difference in your well-being.

Before our first solo tour, Kathlyn spent an evening at a bike shop learning the fundamentals of bike repair and adjustment. Gay, the prototypical mechanical klutz, stayed home that night. One evening was all that it took to learn enough basics to get by. We carry a couple of miniature repair books with us for minor adjustments (one of the best is Rob Van Der Plas' *Roadside Bicycle Repairs*, published by Kampmann and Company; $3.95). Anything more complicated goes to a bike shop. Before riding each day, we always make the following quick checks:

Quick releases. We make sure they are tightened down properly, having learned the hard way that bicycle gremlins can loosen these gadgets while we sleep.

Tire pressure. A squeeze will tell you whether you have the right amount of air in your tire. Keeping tires inflated to their right amount will prevent such common problems as pinched (snake-bit) tubes, as well as keeping you rolling down the road most efficiently.

Brakes. We take a look at the cable to make sure it's still in good shape, then squeeze the brakes a few times to be sure they are grabbing. When bikes come out of the hands of the airlines, the brakes always seem to need a little adjusting. During a tour, brakes seem to need attention every couple of days.

Chains. Keep them lubricated. A tube of Tri-Flow has accompanied us all over the world (not the same one, unfortunately). There are probably other excellent products that do the same thing, but this is the one we always use. A drop on each chain link does it, and should be repeated every few days on a long tour. When your chain gets shiny, it's time for more. We change chains about once a year, more often if it has been a heavy travel year.

Handlebars. Give them a twist in all the relevant directions before you start each day. After having the unsettling but attention-focusing experience of having handlebars come off in our hands a couple of times, we give them a heroic pull up, down, and sideways before riding off.

Derailleurs. We like to shift our gears up and down a few

times in the first few minutes of a ride to be sure they are functioning smoothly. Adjustment of derailleurs is one of the facts of life in the saddle, so might as well do it early in the day.

Seat height and angle. Once you get your seat at the right height and angle you probably will not have to bother with it again. It is worth checking it each day, however, because many sore knees, shoulders, and numb crotches are the result of improper seat adjustment. Get a good bike shop to show you just how to position your seat and its angle to give you the most efficient and comfortable stroke.

WARMING UP: FOUR STRETCHES

We have found that our touring day goes much more smoothly if we take a few minutes to stretch before riding, then take it easy the first mile or two. Warming up is sometimes hard to remember because you will often be excited about setting off on the day's ride. It has been our experience that many of the common complaints, such as aching knees at the end of the day, are the result of starting off too quickly and without a warm-up. The joints of the body contain material that is designed to cushion shock and friction, but to do so efficiently it must be warm. The reason is that the material expands when it is warm, and it is the expansion that gives it its cushioning power. Just as your pillow needs fluffing in the morning after being slept on overnight, your joints need some "fluffing" to get the night's flatness and stiffness out of them. The following stretches will warm your joints slowly and gently. Your first few minutes on the bike should also be slow and gentle. We make it a practice to ride around for five or ten minutes before tackling a big hill first thing in the morning. The older you are, the more important your warm-up is. Both of us are in our forties, but since learning to stretch and warm up properly, we have never missed a day's touring because of soreness or injury. Here are the four easy stretches that we have evolved over the years. We are by no means experts on stretching; these exercises are simply those which

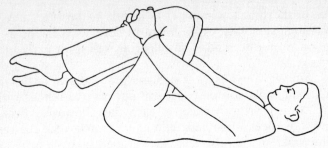

STRETCH NO. 1

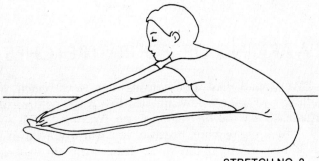

STRETCH NO. 2

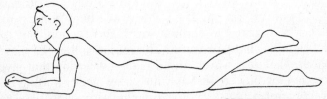

STRETCH NO. 3

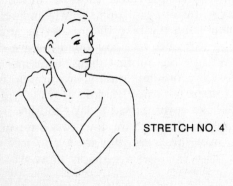

STRETCH NO. 4

have worked for us. If you would like a more formal series of bike stretches, read Bob Anderson's thorough book on the subject, *Stretching* (Shelter Publications; $9.95).

Stretch No. 1: Lie on your back on the floor. Bring your knees up and clasp your arms around them. Breathe deeply and slowly as you rock gently around, massaging your lower back. Keep your stomach muscles relaxed; induce the rocking motion with your hands. Continue for a minute or two, until the low back and sacral area feels warmed up, then stretch out and relax for a little while.

Stretch No. 2: Sit on the floor with your legs stretched out in front of you. Place your hands on your thighs. As you breathe out slowly, lean forward and slide your hands down your legs as far as is comfortable for you. As you breathe in, slide your hands back up your legs. Repeat for a minute or two, in coordination with your breathing. Each time you slide down your legs with your hands, you may notice you go a little farther, although please avoid making a contest out of it.

Stretch No. 3: Lie on your stomach, propping yourself up on your elbows. Breathing slowly and deeply, raise each leg in turn 3–4 inches off the floor. Do these lifts slowly and gently, raising the legs just a few inches and then lowering them.

Stretch No. 4: Take your right hand and grip your left shoulder. Breathing slowly and deeply, turn your head gently from side to side. Turn first toward the side you are holding, then 180 degrees the other direction (or as much as is comfortable). Repeat three times, then switch your grip to the opposite shoulder. After three repetitions, pause in the middle and slowly look up and down three times.

BREATHING FOR PEAK ENDURANCE

Efficient breathing is essential to ending the touring day feeling good. Nature has handed us an obstacle to overcome in this department. When human beings get upset or undergo stress, they move their breathing up into their chests. This fires off the adrenalin machinery, the three-million-year-old fight or flight response. Adrenalin is a powerful stimulant, but it is designed for short bursts only. It is important to stay relaxed and centered as you ride, so that your breathing can stay in your deep abdomen as well as your chest. When the breathing is only in the chest, the heart has to work harder and the blood pressure goes up.

The majority of the blood circulation in your lungs is in the lower third of them, between the bottom of your sternum and your navel. Over a quart of blood circulates down there every minute, as compared with less than a teacup up at the top of your lungs below your collarbone. Many of us keep our bellies tight, forcing the breath up into the chest. Our bodies will work much more efficiently if we can learn to relax our bellies and breathe deeply down into our abdomens. If we could give one universal piece of advice that would make riding more fun, it would be to keep the belly relaxed so that you can breathe deeply down into your abdomen as well as up in your chest. That way, you will be using all the territory that nature has provided inside you. If you would like a tape that details efficient breathing activities, you can send for one that Gay has recorded (*The Art of Breathing and Centering*, available from your favorite bookstore or from Audio Renaissance, 5858 Wilshire Boulevard, Suite 205, Los Angeles, CA 90036; $9.95).

PART TWO

THE FIVE TOURS

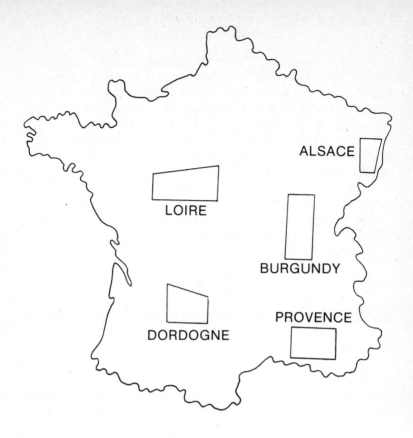

AFTER MANY YEARS OF HAPPY TOURING IN FRANCE, WE
have found that the following five tours are the *crème de la
crème*. Each tour will give you a unique experience of what
France has to offer. In choosing to focus on these five tours,
we have left out a couple of areas that may look good on
paper but have definite disadvantages. You are welcome to
try them out and send us your own evaluations, however; we
are always on the lookout for other people's experiences. For
example, the Riviera is notably missing from our set of tours.
We think the Riviera has simply gotten too dangerous for
happy bike touring. Crowded even in the off-season, the Côte
d'Azur is not well laid out for cycling. Often the main roads
are the only practical ways to get places, which forces you to
expose yourself to cars going sometimes 100–plus miles per

hour. This does not make for serene cycling. The Champagne region is not listed, either. It sounds charming but is actually, in our opinion, a pretty boring place to ride. There's not much to see or do up in that area compared to wonderfully exciting areas like the Dordogne, Loire, or the other three regions we describe. Normandy and Brittany do not make our list, either. Weather is more uncertain in those parts, and the riding is not the most interesting we have found.

The following five tours could keep you busy for several years or a long summer. By the time you exhaust the glories of our Big Five, you will be eager to chart your own territory. We'd love to hear your discoveries.

THE KEYS

There is a key to price in lodging and restaurants. The three categories are *Modest*, *Medium*, and *Top*. Modest refers to lodgings or dinner for two (with one drink apiece) for less than the equivalent of $50. Medium refers to lodgings or dinner for $50–100. Top refers to lodgings or dinner for over $100. Times may change, and events such as devaluation may occur to your favor or not, so please take our key in the spirit in which it was intended: helpful but not carved in stone.

If the price key is not noted, this means that cost is in the Modest range.

Note: Throughout the book, distances are given in miles for several reasons. Most North American readers and cyclists are more accustomed to thinking in miles than kilometers. Some people, we've found, get downright testy about having to translate kilometers into miles. In addition, if you have brought your own bike, chances are your odometer is calibrated in miles. Nearly all of them can be recalibrated into kilometers, but many people do not want to bother to do this. So, miles it will be. French road signs will be in kilometers, which are easy to convert to miles simply by multiplying the kilometer reading times .6. So, for example, 30 kilometers converts to 18 miles, 40 kilometers becomes 24 miles, etc.

CHÂTEAU TO CHÂTEAU:

A CLASSIC TOUR OF

THE LOIRE VALLEY

WELCOME TO A VERDANT LAND OF DELICATE WINES, glorious architecture, and fascinating history. The Loire is called "the garden of France." If this is your first time out, this tour would be a great way to start. Here you will visit quintessential France. A saying you may hear is "Brittany is Brittany and Burgundy is Burgundy, but the Loire Valley is France." The territory is gorgeous and easy to ride, the food among the best in the world, and your lodgings can be as sumptuous or simple as your budget dictates.

On this tour, you will cruise by some of the most breath-taking architecture in all the world. The castles of the Loire, with their patina of age, express a grace and sense of order that is largely missing from the contemporary world. Even if walking through castles is not your thing, you absolutely must take a couple of mornings or afternoons to see how the very wealthy lived (some still do) in these inexpressibly beautiful palaces.

A great deal of rich history has taken place along the Loire, France's longest river. The Romans once held sway here, and the people of the Loire were the first in France to rebel against the reign of Caesar. Later, other invaders, such as the Huns and Norsemen from the north and the Moors from the east, plundered the riches of the Loire Valley. In the twelfth century, the Plantagenets ruled their vast territories from this area. At one point they commanded an empire that stretched from the Pyrenees to the Scottish Highlands.

You will be able to walk through the château at Chinon where Joan of Arc was entrusted with the command of the army by Charles VII. You can stand on the spot where the Chevalier King Francis I welcomed his guest from Italy, Leonardo da Vinci, whom he had imported as an artist-in-residence. You may take a turn around a ballroom where Catherine de Medici played hostess to the cream of French society.

Along the river you will see escarpments of tufa, the unusual rock which dominates the architecture of the region. Tufa is a pale stone which turns whiter as it ages. The French have a knack for creating art that grows more beautiful with time, and nowhere is this striking skill more apparent than in the Loire Valley. If you can take your eyes away from the châteaux for a moment, you will see tiny cottages made from the same stone, which, when capped by the black slate roofs of the region, fall very gracefully on the eye.

THE CUISINE AND WINES OF THE LOIRE

The Loire has been such a melting pot of French culture over the years that it cannot be said to have a specific cuisine of its own. It has absorbed the best of all French cooking. You may encounter a truffled omelette that will make you swear you are in the Dordogne. At another meal you may eat a young duckling simmered in a rich Burgundian wine sauce with mushrooms. Freshwater fish occupies a prominent place on the table here. You might be fortunate, as we were, to happen upon a tiny inn where the owner was walking up with a pike that he had caught a few minutes earlier. Soon his wife had turned it into a small masterpiece of loving cookery, baking the succulent fish in a flaky jacket of puff pastry and serving it with an assortment of just-picked garden vegetables.

Cheese lovers will be happy here, especially if you like the earthy goat cheeses. Among the most famous is Crottin de Chavignol. *Crottin* translates as "horse dung," which fortunately refers to the appearance, not the taste, of this cheese. Not everyone likes goat cheese, though. M. F. K. Fisher, the great food writer, was of the opinion that goat cheese tasted like "cheese with dirt," and if you share this opinion you will find a luscious array of cow's-milk cheeses to choose from. The authors do not number goat cheese among their passions; one of the first French phrases we learned was *pas de chèvre, s'il vous plaît*, which translates as "no goat cheese, please."

The Loire Valley is justly famous for its light wines. The delicious Vouvray is born here, as are the flowery red Touraine and its white cousin. If your taste is for rosé, one of the finest, rosé d'Anjou, issues from the Loire. The dry, fresh Muscadet and the distinguished Sancerre are also unique to this region. You will not go thirsty, or hungry, in the Loire.

SAUMUR

The Loire tour begins in the town of Saumur, whose main buildings overlook the Loire River. Saumur is reached by train from Paris. Trains leave the Gare d'Austerlitz every hour or two all day long; you may have to change trains at Tours for the smaller town. Saumur is surprisingly sophisticated for a town with a medieval heart. It blends cosmopolitan charm and ancient solidity, and reminded us of a Swiss city. The fourteenth-century château whose towers dominate the town is widely regarded as one of the finest in the Loire Valley; you will pass it as you begin riding. Containing a museum now, the château was once used as a prison by Napoleon. Horse lovers will also find a museum devoted to the horse, which has played a prominent role in the history of the town. Even today the town's riding club is well known wherever horsey people congregate. Saumur is definitely worth a leisurely stroll around town. The market vendors have gorgeous fruits and vegetables for sale in season.

The town has both modern shops and an old section with fascinating architecture. The office of tourism is well stocked. We suggest you stop there to pick up maps and information for additional activities, such as balloon rides in the area.

WHERE TO STAY AND DINE IN SAUMUR

If your budget permits, splurge and stay at the wonderful Hostellerie du Prieuré, on the outskirts of town, four miles from the center of Saumur on the D751 (Chênehutte-les-Tuffeaux; tel. 41–67–90–14). Well worth its high prices, this fifteenth-century restoration rests in the center of its own sixty-acre grounds. Comfort lovers will appreciate the heated pool, as well as the concoctions of the chef. (Top) If you would like to dine in town, try the Restaurant Le Gambetta (12 rue Gambetta; tel. 41–67–66–66), where you will dine on a variety of local fish and an outstanding array of desserts. Worth the long wait is that pinnacle of desserts, the soufflé, done here in the grand style. (Modest)

You will find Le Roi René (94 avenue du General de Gaulle, 49400 Saumur; tel. 41–67–45–30), in a quiet area of town overlooking the Loire. Redecorated and with new plumbing, each room has a private bath and lots of light. The restaurant is reasonable and has good local cuisine. (Modest)

DAY ONE: SAUMUR TO CHINON

We've chosen this short route of about 20 miles today to give you a chance to get acclimated to your bicycle in this territory and to show you a representative sample of the Loire region. You'll see clusters of medieval villages, vineyards, and rolling farmlands. The ride is short, but over each rise you will discover a different world.

Begin your ride at the tourist office and ride east along the Loire. (sign: Fontevraud) You will pass the château on your right, along with many little shops and cafés. The road is level and tree-lined in this first section.

At D205, turn right at the village of **Souzay-Champigny.** (signs: Champigny, Chace) Ride through the little village of Souzay to enter the vineyards of Saumur, highly regarded in France but not widely known in the United States.

In **Champigny** fork left on D145.

Fork left again in a few hundred feet to stay on D145. (sign: Fontevraud) Be on the lookout for blackberry bushes. The road winds downhill through deep woods, then gently uphill. Stay on D145, which leads you through one of the most lushly forested areas in the region. Approaching Fontevraud you'll encounter a fairly steep hill, then several hills and dales just before you enter the town.

In **Fontevraud** take D947 toward Montsoreau.

Turn right at Abbaye Royale. (sign: Couziers)
This eleventh-century abbey holds the tombs of the early Plantagenets and it's worth stopping to tour its romanesque architecture.

At fork past the abbey walls, go left. (signs: VC4, Couziers, Circuit des Moutiers) You'll make a short, steep climb along vine-covered walls past an old church, where you'll keep bearing right. On the day we last rode this route, the only other vehicle we encountered was a lone bicycle racer.

At the junction in front of Galerie des Moutiers, go left. (sign: Chinon)

After about 100 yards, at a Y fork, go right toward Lerné. You'll ride through hay fields to a stop sign.

Turn left on D117. (sign: Lerné)

At the next fork, bear right toward Chinon (not toward Lerné Centre). On your right you'll pass the stone houses of the farming village of Lerné, still steeped in the Middle Ages.

Follow the signs to Chinon. About 6 miles from Chinon, look to your right and note the château on the hill.

At the first stop sign in the village of **Seuilly,** go straight. **Go left on D24.** (sign: Chinon) In this section of the ride there are many wine cellars and tasting opportunities, including the Caves de Grenelle and Gratien et Meyer.

Turn left on D759, leaving the village of **La Roche-Clermault.** (sign: Chinon)

At the roundabout follow signs to Chinon Centre. The last few miles into Chinon may have traffic, but the road has an excellent shoulder.

At the next roundabout, go right on D749. You'll come into **Chinon** with the Vienne River on your right. Look up to your left as you enter town, and you'll see the ramparts of the old château.

WHERE TO STAY AND DINE IN CHINON

There is a wide variety of inexpensive hotels along the quai de Jeanne d'Arc, which fronts on the river, but having spent a noisy night in one of them, we recommend avoiding this heavily trafficked thoroughfare. Quieter possibilities, centrally located, are:

Chris' Hôtel (12 place Jeanne-d'Arc, 37500 Chinon; tel. 47–93–36–92). This comfortable hotel, with its classic facade, has forty rooms decorated in Louis XV style, a quiet outdoor courtyard, its own dining room, direct telephones, and bathrooms with showers or bath. (Modest)

Hôtel de France (47–49, place du General de Gaulle, 37500 Chinon; tel. 47–93–33–91). This more modern hotel is located right off the *centre ville*. Merchants were selling a variety of fresh fruits and vegetables in the square opposite the hotel one day. This hotel's rooms come with bath or shower and telephone. The hotel has a lounge, and is very close to several good restaurants. From this hotel you have just a short walk to the château. (Modest)

Hôtel Diderot (4 rue Buffon and 7 rue Diderot, 37500 Chinon; tel. 47–93–18–87). Our personal favorite, the Hôtel Diderot is a restored eighteenth-century house built around a courtyard. The three-storied vine-covered stone building has twenty very clean rooms with direct telephones. Our room had beamed ceilings and tiled floors (although some rooms are wallpapered) with antique furniture, and the bathrooms are beautifully tiled. Most important, the bed was wonderfully firm (the French often seem to favor roll-to-the-middle soft-ness), and the reading lamps packed sufficient wattage that we didn't have to bring out our flashlights. The hosts were very amiable and helpful with information about local sights and directions. The hotel has no restaurant, but they do serve breakfast—with their own homemade jams. (Modest)

Restaurant Le Sainte-Maxime (31 place du General de Gaulle, 37500 Chinon; tel. 47–93–05–04). The first good sign was the crowd of locals on a weeknight, necessitating our sharing a table with a friendly German couple who told us about the beauties of Provence. The next clue was the exten-sive menu and wine list. After considerable study of our menu translator, we selected an excellent chef's salad with endive, gruyère, and chicken, and their special *coq au vin*. The service was quick, prices reasonable, and the waiters took time to help us translate. (Modest)

There are several pleasant cafés and restaurants sur-rounding the *centre ville* square. We found it very easy to eat lightly or sumptuously. One popular restaurant, Jeanne de France, served pizza and crepes from a huge menu where 75 francs ($12.50) purchased pizza, an entrée soup, and a *crêpe au chocolat*. Lots of fresh vegetables, and excellent salads and soups were available everywhere.

WHAT TO SEE AND DO IN CHINON

The best view of Chinon is reputedly (and in our experience) from across the Vienne, where you may enjoy taking a morning ride to explore the shops and wineries. This area tends to be less crowded than the central streets.

You'll be able to tour Chinon easily on foot. Do climb up to the château, which has a long history beginning as a fortification in Roman times. You enter the château through a clock tower which features a Joan of Arc museum. There is a model of the château inside one of the three fortifications, and you will enjoy the expansive views, especially from the south walls. Until the mid-1400s, Chinon was a royal residence. The castle has recently been restored by the government. Just outside the château is a small café perched on the hill where you can enjoy the sights and cuisine of the area.

We took our bikes on a tour of the winding streets of Chinon and found little *boulangeries* (bakeries) tucked away on side streets, immaculately tended houses and gardens, and many friendly people. Chinon is typical of Loire Valley villages, with its narrow streets and stone houses built up the hill. You may find such an unmitigated profusion of beauty that, as we did, you begin dreaming of the villages and country roads at night.

SUMMARY

LOIRE TOUR: DAY ONE

Saumur to Chinon

(approximately 20 miles)

- Leave Saumur by going east along the Loire for 3½ miles.
- Turn right onto D205 for 1 mile.
- In Champigny fork left on D145 and ride a little over 4 miles.

- Turn onto D947 toward Montsoreau in Fontevraud.
- Turn right at Abbaye Royale and left at the fort past the abbey walls (signs: VC4, Couziers).
  There is a short, steep climb here past an old church.
- At the junction in front of Galerie des Moutiers, go left (sign: Chinon).
- After about 100 yards, at a Y fork, go right toward Lerné. You'll ride through hay fields about 4 miles to the next junction.
- Turn left on D117 (sign: Lerné).
- Bear right toward Chinon at the next fork, not Lerné Centre.
- You will notice a château on your right, which indicates about 8 more miles into Chinon.
- In Seuilly go straight at the first stop sign.
- Turn left on D24 (sign: Chinon).
- After approximately 1½ miles, go left on D759, as you exit the village of La Roche-Clermault.
- At the roundabout, follow signs to Chinon Centre. Use the excellent shoulder on this busy stretch for almost 2 miles.
- At the next roundabout, go right on D749.
- Signs will lead you the short couple of miles into Chinon.

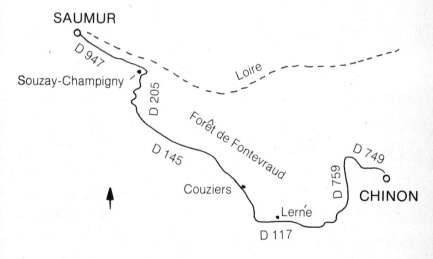

DAY TWO: CHINON TO VILLANDRY

Today's tour will give your legs a chance to stretch out by covering about 40 miles of exquisite countryside. Begin today pedaling east on the quai Jeanne d'Arc along the Vienne River.

Just outside town, turn onto the D8. (sign: L'Île-Bouchard) The smooth, fairly flat road passes through meadows and under a canopy of shade trees. Along the way you'll pass several wine châteaux, where you may want to stop and buy a bottle for lunch later. Vineyards line the road all the way in the first section. (If you want a more challenging ride, take the D21 out of Chinon. It covers roughly the same territory but is further up the slopes.)

Take the tiny V5 left. (sign: Panzoult) This road heads up through cornfields and gives you more of the view of the slopes in the area.

At the T intersection in Panzoult turn right. (There is a bar and tobacco shop here.)

After a block go left on D21. (sign: Azay-le-Rideau) Now you are riding away from the Vienne River, and the road becomes more hilly as it winds through grape country dotted with pretty farm houses.

Cross the busy D757.

Turn left on the D138. (sign: Avon les Roches) After leaving the pretty village of **Avon les Roches,** the road angles uphill for a little over a mile, then levels out as it passes through a military base. From there the road is straight as an arrow with a slight uphill grade and the signs turn into D132.

A few miles outside of Azay the road turns hilly as you pass through a section of the Forêt de Chinon, groves of oak and beech interspersed with orange and purple pines.

At the fork, turn right on D757. This long uphill takes you to some prime blackberry bushes where you can refresh yourself in season before heading downhill again.

Turn right on D751a into Azay-le-Rideau for lunch. We enjoyed a light meal in La Salamandre, an outdoor café just off the flower-bedecked *centre ville*. There is a *boulangerie* for picnic supplies and several more formal restaurants, such as Le Balzac and La Renaissance.

Follow the signs to the château. Nestled among the lush meadows of the Indre River, this small château is considered a jewel among the Loire castles. Built between 1518 and 1529 by the king's wealthy treasurer, this castle is loaded with period status symbols. It is partly moated, topped by towers and parapets, engineered with the latest in grand staircases, and even comes complete with machicolations, those handy openings for dumping hot oil or heavy objects on your enemies. The interior also reflects the values of the time, which unfortunately did not include creature comforts. The blocky rooms are very cold and drafty, the doors invite wind, and the fireplaces would not pass current inspection, much less provide much heat. Even the lush setting was somewhat hazardous, as the Indre flooded several times. The floors were finally elevated in the nineteenth century.

Leave Azay-le-Rideau toward Villandry on the busy D757. You'll traverse a steep hill for about ½ mile. We've designed this afternoon route to show you a more rural way into Villandry.

Turn left on D39. This quiet road undulates through apple orchards, vineyards, and cornfields.
In **Vallères**, you'll pass a tower on your right as you cycle on the narrow roads of this village.

Turn onto VI. (sign: Druye) If you see a church on your right, you've gone too far. Stay on the main road, which bends right about ½ mile outside of town. You'll pedal past sunflower fields, then uphill through a beautiful wooded area where we encountered little traffic. You'll emerge into farmland.

At this junction turn left. (If you look back over your shoulder, the sign on the west side of the street says Villandry.) At a house with an orchard in front on the way to Villandry you'll go gently uphill for approximately a mile. The remainder of this section is downhill.

At a Y fork in the middle of the fields, veer right.

At the T intersection, go left onto D121. You should coast into **Villandry** within 4 miles.

WHERE TO STAY AND DINE IN VILLANDRY

Your choice in Villandry is very simple. Le Cheval Rouge is *the* hotel (37510 Joué-les-Tours; tel. 47–50–02–07). Fortunately, it is a two-star establishment whose twenty rooms all have baths or showers. The hotel restaurant serves regional specialties such as fish from the Loire, and the chef is particularly proud of his pastries. (Medium)

If you like, bicycle a mile and a half past Villandry where there is another bar and hotel on the river. Across from the hotel is a tree-shaded lane that goes down to a picnic area. It is a pleasant place to take a late-afternoon ride. For snacking and picnics, you'll find supplies at the *boulangerie* and *pâtisserie* facing the church.

WHAT TO SEE AND DO IN VILLANDRY

The singular attraction of this tiny town is the Renaissance château, only outshown by its magnificent and extensive gardens. Completed in the early 1500s, the château's architects extended their renown with the completion of the main courtyard. The château houses a fine painting collection, and you can also view a slide show of the gardens' seasons. The gardens themselves are three-tiered and merit hours of exploration of their *Alice in Wonderland* labyrinths. One tier is really a water garden with ponds and pools that reflect the château. Another tier houses a comprehensive and decorative vegetable garden. The third level holds the carefully tended flower garden. Its prime feature, aside from following the theme of love so popular in those chivalrous times, are the box hedges and yews which offer some protection from the winds.

Several miles down the D7 toward Tours are the Grottoes of Savonnières. Two grottoes have been discovered, both full of unusual formations, stalactites, pools, and cascades. The grottoes also house an interesting petrified museum which displays lithographic sculptures from the nineteenth century.

SUMMARY

LOIRE TOUR: DAY TWO

Chinon to Villandry

(approximately 40 miles)

- Start today pedaling east on the quai Jeanne d'Arc along the Vienne River for a few hundred feet.
- Turn onto the D8 just outside Chinon and ride for about 8½ miles.
- Take the tiny V5 left (sign: Panzoult).
- After less than a mile, at the T intersection in Panzoult, turn right.
- After a block go left on D21 for a little less than 2 miles. Cross the busy D757.
- Turn left on the D138 (sign: Avon les Roches). Ride for 8½ miles through forests and blackberry bushes.
- At the fork, turn right on D757 and ride for 3½ miles.
- Turn right on D751a into Azay-le-Rideau for lunch.
- Leave Azay on the busy D757 toward Villandry.
- After ½ mile, turn left on D39.
- After about 3 miles you'll come into Vallères and a series of rural turns.
- Turn onto V1 (sign: Druye) and ride for about 3 miles.
- At the next junction, in a farmland, turn left. You'll cycle through farmland for about 3 miles.
- At a Y fork in the middle of the field, veer right.
- At the T intersection, go left onto D121.
- You should coast into Villandry within 4 miles.

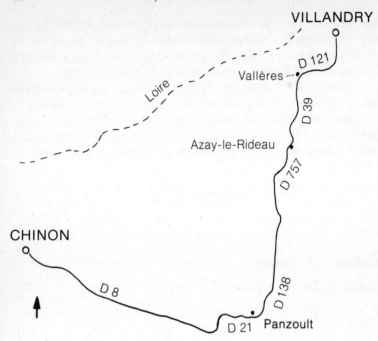

DAY THREE: VILLANDRY TO CHENONCEAUX

We've outlined a roundabout route to Chenonceaux to stay on the prettiest rural roads and avoid the congestion of Tours. Today's route covers 40 mostly flat miles. We are assuming that you are taking this trip by bicycle to enjoy the pleasures of France at a more leisurely pace that gives all your senses a chance to expand and relax: Hence the back roads.

Begin today's tour by traveling east from the front of Le Cheval Rouge on the D7. (sign: Balan-Miré) You'll pass little villages along the river Cher, with many photo opportunities of the serene river scenes.

At the far end of **Savonnières,** you'll come to a junction with a choice to take the D7 to Tours. Turn right instead on the rue du Paradis.

You'll immediately see C8, which indicates that you're on the right road. (sign: Balan) Keep following the signs toward Balan-Miré. The road meanders through fields and forests with some scattered blackberry bushes.

At the T junction in **Miré** (sign: V7 to Balan), go right at the sign that says Chinon-Tours. You will cross railroad tracks and the busy D751.

Continue on D8 (signs: Artannes, Sache, Thilouze).
This section is delightfully filled with the soft air, muted colors, and meadows and fields characteristic of the Loire.

Turn left at sign to Artannes. (sign: rue des Lambert Champ)

Turn left again in about two blocks.

Go left on the D17 in the middle of **Artannes**. (sign: Monts) You'll see and may want to stop at the château of Artannes on your left.

Our experiences in Tours and other large cities like it have strengthened our determination to avoid them on bicycles. The congestion and traffic are an unpleasant shock after the peaceful, unhurried country roads and small villages. If you feel the need to visit Tours, your opportunity is coming up with the D86 junction in **Monts.**

To take the alternate route into Tours, turn left on D86. (sign: Tours)
If you are not too tired on arriving in Tours, you might enjoy a stroll around the town's major attraction, the Cathedral of St.-Gatien. You will marvel at the stained glass windows, some of which have been there for eight hundred years. The old district of the city is good for a walk, as are the university environs. If you would like an overview of the Loire Valley you are about to see, visit the Historial de Touraine museum at the Château Royal, quai d'Orléans. The history of the area

is depicted in scenes and wax figures covering the last thousand years.

WHERE TO STAY AND DINE IN TOURS

If you want to be close to the center of Tours, you can comfortably settle into one of Tours' numerous pleasant hotels. We recommend the Meridien (292 avenue de Grammont; tel. 37–28–00–80) or Le Royal (65 avenue de Grammont; tel. 47–64–71–78), both of which are in the Medium category. The Meridien has pretty grounds, with a garden and swimming pool; Le Royal offers its guests tastefully decorated rooms with antique furnishings and modern facilities.

   In our opinion, the best place to stay is a few miles outside Tours in the village of Joué-les-Tours. Leave the city on D86 (the road you rode in on), then take D207 toward Beaulieu. There you will find the lovely Château de Beaulieu (tel. 47–53–20–26). In quiet seclusion 5 miles away from the bustle of the city, this hotel rates three stars but is still in the Medium price category. The restaurant is also superb. In the Medium range, you will dine sumptuously, with the chef's prize *foie gras* and a selection of transcendent desserts. The Château also has tennis courts and a swimming pool available for guests. It does not have many rooms, so reservations are highly recommended. (Modest–Medium)

To rejoin the tour, return on the D86 to **Monts**, then turn left on the D17.

Keep following the signs toward Montbazon. You will ride under the A10 autoroute overpass in woodland country, with the Indre River to your left.

At the X intersection with N6 (at the Hôtel de Ville), turn left. (sign: Veigne) This is a busy commercial intersection where we suggest you stop for lunch. There is a variety of *brasseries*, restaurants, and *boulangeries*. If no particular decor inspires you, we suggest shopping for picnic supplies for a riverside luncheon further down the road.

After several long blocks on the N6, turn right on the D17. (sign: Veigne) Stay on the D17 through **Esvres**. The Indre is on your right now as you pedal through river valley country.

At the next junction, head right. (sign: Loches) You'll still be on the D17 as you move gently uphill into fertile Loire farmland.

At the junction with N143, turn right. (sign: Cormery)

Escape to your left onto D45. (sign: Bléré) This road is smooth and flat. It snakes through open fields and the charming village of **Athée sur Cher.**

Follow the signs to your right, toward Bléré. You'll still be on the D45.

At the N76 junction, go right. (sign: Bléré)

Head left at the Toutes Directions sign and ride through town.

Turn left toward Amboise and Chenonceaux. Cross the bridge over the Cher.

At the X stoplight junction in **La Croix**, turn right. (Sign: Chenonceaux) Ride through **Civray de Touraine**.

Head right on the D40. (sign: Chenonceaux, which will be on your right)

WHERE TO STAY AND DINE IN CHENONCEAUX

The French have conveniently provided accommodations right next to the château. There is an intersection with several clustered choices competing for the tourist dollar.

The Hôtel du Bon Laboureur et du Château (37150 Chenonceaux; tel. 47–23–90–02). The elegant simplicity of this three-star, old hotel (established in 1800) makes it *the* place to stay. We were impressed by the true sense of France in the flower-bedecked and warm wood decor, the friendliness of the staff, and their commitment to preserving traditions and cuisine handed down through generations.

You will recognize it by its ivy-covered walls and rose gardens, and will be well taken care of by the owner and his wife, M. and Mme. Jeudi. The restaurant offers comfortable, hearty dining in an attractively furnished room. In good weather, you may want to eat outside under the maple tree in the courtyard. M. Jeudi doubles as chef, and he has two menus for you to choose from. The first, in the Modest range, may offer you his *rillettes*, a dish of spicy ground pork. If this is on the menu, we highly recommend it. For the Medium price, you can have his *menu gastronomique*, which may feature a seafood dish or sweetbreads simmered in wine sauce. Even if you have a prejudice against the obscure organs that so delight French chefs, try the sweetbreads (*ris de veau*). You will be stocking up on much-needed protein and vitamin B12 for tomorrow's ride.

The rooms have telephones and private bathrooms. If you travel during the summer you can enjoy your meals in the gardens. One couple reported coming to stay for one day and remaining five; we understood. (Medium)

The Hôtel Ottoni (37150 Chenonceaux; tel. 47–23–90–09). This three-star, pleasant, two-story hotel also has its own restaurant. When we visited, the courtyard café was full of diners enjoying both the food and the view of cascading flowers from the balcony. (Modest)

The Hôtellerie du Lion d'Argent (37150 Chenonceaux; tel. 47–23–90–31). This hotel and restaurant is built around a stone courtyard. The atmosphere was more private and reserved here, which may be just the thing after jostling through crowds at the château. (Modest)

WHAT TO SEE AND DO IN CHENONCEAUX

The château at Chenonceaux is on everyone's "must see" list, as the large parking lot and government-operated food stands outside the entrance attest. Our skepticism about hype was immediately dispelled by the stunning canopy of plane trees we walked under to enter the castle grounds. One of our favorite sustaining images of France is the light through those trees.

Chenonceaux is another Renaissance château, built in 1520 by yet another treasurer (Thomas Bohier, financier to three kings). The château has a rich and dramatic history, and is still privately owned. Many feel that this is the greatest of all the châteaux, here. Inside, you can tour a few floors of the château and study the intricate Gobelin tapestries which provided some warmth to the inhabitants.

When you emerge into the area where the walkways and buildings are, you will understand why this château has one of the most famous settings in the world, poised as it is out over the Cher River. You can imagine Diane de Poitiers' distress at having to relinquish this gem to Henry II's widow, Catherine de Medici. Diane was exiled to Chaumont, while Catherine became even more famous for her entertainments.

In addition to the buildings, there are two gardens—the dueling gardens of Diane and Catherine—on the sides of the château, where you can wander, smell the deep forest smells, and hear the echo of past revelry.

SUMMARY

LOIRE TOUR: DAY THREE

Villandry to Chenonceaux

(35–40 miles)

- Begin today on the D7, traveling east 1½ miles from the front of the hotel Le Cheval Rouge.
- At the far end of Savonnières, turn right on the rue du Paradis. You'll immediately see the sign C8, letting you know you're on the right track.
- Keep following the signs toward Balan-Miré. The road meanders through fields and forests for about 3 miles.
- At the X junction in Miré (sign: V7 to Balan), turn right at the sign

that says Chinon-Tours. You will cross railroad tracks and the busy D751.

- Continue on D8 for a little over 3½ miles.
- Turn left at the sign to Artannes.
- Go left again in about 2 blocks.
- Turn left on the D17 in the middle of Artannes (sign: Monts). You'll stay on D17 for over 13 miles, with a short detour for lunch.
- Follow the signs to Montbazon.
- At the X intersection with N6, turn left. Lunch stop.
- After several long blocks on the N6 turn right on the D17 again, staying on D17 through Esvres.
- At the junction with N143, turn right (sign: Cormery) for a few hundred yards.
- Escape to your left onto D45 (sign: Bléré) for about 5½ miles.
- At the N76 junction, go right (sign: Bléré).
- After a little over a mile, head left at the Toutes Directions sign.
- Turn left toward Amboise and Chenonceaux, crossing the Cher River.
- At the X stoplight junction in La Croix (less than a mile), turn right.
- Head right on the D40 for 4 miles (sign: Chenonceaux, which will be on your right).

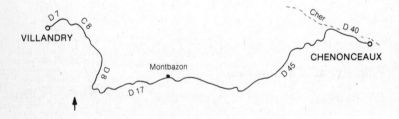

DAYS FOUR AND FIVE: CHENONCEAUX TO CHAMBORD

This is definitely the day of the châteaux. Your morning ride will take you through Amboise to Chaumont for lunch and castle viewing. The long (30 miles) but relatively flat afternoon ride ends in the spacious rooms of Chambord.

The morning's ride will take you to the town of Amboise, 15 miles from Tours. This town was the final home of Leonardo da Vinci, and you will find many mementoes of his presence if you take time to stroll around the ancient town. The Château of Amboise, which dominates the town, has a rich history and commanding views of the Loire Valley. It is open every day (though closed for two hours at noon). Ready for refreshment? If you are really hungry, stop at the Auberge du Mail, outside of town toward Tours. Otherwise you will find a *boulangerie* or two with a fresh loaf of bread waiting for you, to sustain you until Chaumont.

Outside of Chenonceaux château, go left on the D40.

In Civray de Touraine, turn right on D81. (sign: Amboise) You'll be warming up today through gentle hills and vales with even more blackberry hedges and then a gentle uphill.

Turn left at this intersection. (sign: Amboise) Follow the signs to Amboise Centre, where you get a great view of the châteaux from the bridge. Amboise, the burial place of Leonardo da Vinci, has a blend of cosmopolitan and country ambiance, with many streets winding down to the quai General de Gaulle on the Loire River. Several streets are one-way, and the signs are sometimes confusing, so ask if you can't find the château or tourist information center. We definitely recommend a stop at Amboise's tourist center, as it is one of the best equipped we found. We got several good maps there and a publication called *Centre-Val de Loire, Châteaux Country*, which gives times and cost of events, diverse information about all the châteaux and museums in the Loire Valley, and includes many gorgeous photographs. Amboise also seemed to have more shops than many other château towns, so you may want to stroll around before continuing the day's ride.

The château is one of the most imposing of the Renaissance castles, built during the fifteenth and sixteenth centuries, the city's prime. During its history it has been used as a

prison as well as a royal residence, and after the French Revolution parts of it were torn down. One of the best features of
the château is the view it affords from the terrace. You will
also marvel at the two towers, one of which comes complete
with a spiral ramp to accommodate horses, and the other with
massively thick walls.

We have given you two routes to Chaumont, the direct route
and the more leisurely, country route.

THE DIRECT ROUTE

Continue on the quai General-de-Gaulle, the D751. (sign:
Chaumont-sur-Loire) You'll see many vegetable gardens, old
stone walls, and a profusion of flowers as you head out of
Amboise right along the riverbank. There are several wine
cellars in and just outside of town and another castle, the
Château de Pays. You'll remain on the D751 all the way to
Chaumont, which takes you through semiforested area then
out along the Loire again.

ALTERNATE ROUTE

**A little over two miles from Amboise on the D751, between
two old stone walls you'll turn right onto D80 to Souvigny de
Touraine.**

Turn left on D23 to Valliers-les-Grandes.

Turn left again on D28.

Head right on D27.

Intersect with D751 and go right into Chaumont-sur-Loire.
We recommend stopping for lunch at the Hostellerie du Château, right across from the château on D751. We were re-
freshed by the tablecloths, fresh gladioli, waiters who
understood some English, and customs which allowed our bicycling clothing (which the other diners politely ignored). The

restaurant's high, beamed ceilings are supported by wooden pillars from which two deer heads gazed upon us. The dark wood contrasted with white stone walls, and two large French windows opening on the terrace café provided light. A ripe tomato accented the salmon salad. We had the *escargot* and the fresh catch of the day grilled with a sauce of capers. The food and service were excellent.

THE CHÂTEAU AT CHAUMONT

As you climb to the château you'll first encounter the luxurious horse stables, decorated with friezes and probably warmer than most human lodgings of the time. Continue climbing through thick cedar and chestnut trees to reach the château, built between 1465 and 1510 on the strategic site of prior fortifications. The château is in Renaissance style with medieval touches such as covered walks. Its initial defensive, armed look was later softened by replacing the windows and removing the river side of the château, which also opened the view from the courtyard area. You may experience the view as the best part of your climb.

Your afternoon ride is long but relatively flat, taking you into some of the best country roads and sights. You'll glide through mile after mile of unfolding surprises: lush fields, and impeccably tended châteaux and farmhouses.

Begin by taking the D114 uphill with the Chaumont château to your right. The road quickly flattens out through fields for about two miles.

Turn left toward Valaire. Your turn will be just before a line of forest. (signs: Valaire, Sambin, La Probilière)

After one mile, at a three-fork intersection, go right. (sign: Sambin) The smooth road of this section curves through vineyards and fields of sunflowers. Take the next fork toward Sambin.

In Sambin you'll come to an intersection where you'll turn left.

There'll be another intersection just after the town center. Go right on D52 at the monument to local war dead. (signs: Fougères, Bièvres 3k) Continue on D52 past wonderful old farmhouses into the bustling town of **Fougères**, which has a charming church.

At the three-fork intersection in front of the church take the middle road (the path of moderation). (signs: Fresnes, Contres, Cour-Cheverny) You'll be immediately arrested by many lovely houses along the stream.

After just 100 yards or so, you'll take first a left fork then a right one to stay on D52. (sign: Cour-Cheverny) Continue on D52 through **Favras** and through the D956 intersection. Signs will point you to the château at Cheverny. If you go, you'll find one of the few châteaux still owned by the original lineage, the vicomte de Sigalas. The château was built in 1634, in a short period of time. When the vicomte found his wife *in flagrante delicto*, he killed her and her lover, burned the first château, and built a second for his second wife. Both survived, and the second château has been maintained largely in its original state, complete with a large hunting museum—impressive (if two thousand antlers impress you). In the rooms that are open to tour, you'll have the opportunity to view more Gobelins tapestry, the classic Louis XIII architecture, a highly decorative fireplace, and a collection of medieval armor. Perhaps the nicest aspect of the château is the garden: there are lovely streams and ponds among the trees.

If you elected to visit the château, retrace your path to the D52, and remain on this road into **Cour-Cheverny.** In Cour-Cheverny you may choose to restock your blood sugar at their excellent *boulangerie*.

At the next intersection, turn right toward Bracieux. (sign: Centre Ville)

In the *centre ville*, turn left on D102. (sign: Bracieux)

At the light, go straight. (signs: Bracieux, Paris) Liver lovers take note: you can buy *foie gras* directly from a roadside farmhouse in this section.

In **Tour-en-Sologne**, take D102 to the right. (sign: Chambord)

Turn right at the next intersection on D102. (sign: Bracieux) Ride on into **Bracieux** and follow the Toutes Directions signs through town.

Turn left at the sign that says Chambord.

Another left at the sign for Blois, Chambord.

Follow this with a right. (sign: Chambord)

Cross the Beuvron.

Take a right fork on D112. (sign: Chambord)
You'll pedal on a wide, straight road through the deep Forest of Boulogne, where we especially appreciated the speed of bicycling. You'll enter the gates of the Parc de Chambord, surrounded by what is said to be the longest wall in France—32 kilometers. You'll see acres of oak as you approach the village and château.

WHERE TO STAY AND DINE IN CHAMBORD

The Hôtel du St.-Michel (103 place Saint-Michel, Chambord 41250 Bracieux; tel. 54–20–31–31) is not only in a desirable location right across from the château; it is the only hotel in Chambord. The overall feel of the hotel is provincial, clean, and efficient. The outside of the hotel is especially charming, hung with vines and bougainvillea. (Modest)

Le Chambourdin (route de Bracieux, 4159 Chambord; tel. 54–20–32–64), a restaurant and bar, is in the village southwest of the château. We enjoyed some crusty French bread, excellent country pâté, and local fresh vegetables in their Swiss-style dining room.

We recommend staying two nights and either exploring the miniature city of Chambord in detail, or taking a side trip into Blois, which you can reach directly on the D33. The château at Blois is justly famous, having received the architectural attention of counts and kings over several centuries. The Blois château is considered the zenith of Renaissance construction and ornamentation and was the site of several significant historical events, including the murder by Henry III of his rival, the Duke of Guise. The château's rooms are still being restored (having also suffered during the Revolution and after), but its staircases, courtyard, and various wings are well worth the trip.

A pleasant and reasonable night's lodging, should you choose to stay the second night in Blois, is available at Anne de Bretagne on avenue J.-Laigret (tel. 54–78–05–38). This small rose-covered inn is spotless and comfortable. (Modest)

Our recommendation for dinner is La Péniche (tel. 54–74–37–23). Here you will have an intimate experience of the Loire: La Péniche is a barge which floats on the river's right bank. The seafood is uniformly excellent here, and the owner, M. Bosque, also has a way with mushrooms and truffles. You will find a wide range of items available here. (Medium)

Another dining option in Blois is to go outside of town toward Tours about 2 miles on the N152. Here you will find L'Espérance (tel. 54–78–09–01), a richly decorated and quiet room with great views of the Loire. You might have a simple omelette with truffles that will be better than any omelette you have ever tasted. Or you might, with luck, arrive on a night when the duckling is accompanied by morels. If you stick with set price dinners you will stay in the Medium range, but if you order à la carte you may stray into the Top bracket. The restaurant is not open for dinner on Sunday and closed all day Monday. (Medium–Top)

WHAT TO SEE AND DO IN CHAMBORD

No pictures can quite prepare you for the enormity of Chambord. It's as if thirty-two architects engaged in a simultaneous competition, resulting in over 440 rooms, a profusion of towers, a famous double staircase, turrets, parapets, and embellishments of all sorts. Francis I, beginning in 1519 and continuing for twenty years, did not stint in any way in constructing the largest château in the Loire Valley. In fact, the Loire itself was diverted to enhance the château's effect. History was made here, Molière's plays were performed here for the Sun King, and gentlemen chased their mistresses up and down the double spiral staircase designed by Leonardo da Vinci. This ostentatious royal display was ransacked during the Revolution and all its furnishings destroyed. Before the government acquired it in 1932, it had been a munitions factory. The château has four enormous towers, vaulted ceilings, highly decorated windows, and chimneys in every direction. The château is nicely framed by the six gates that open onto its six avenues.

You will know you are in an "official" tourist site because of the large parking lot and the avenue of souvenir shops, which are actually well stocked with maps and regional information. The site also houses a wine shop specializing in the wines of the Cher and Loire region.

SUMMARY

LOIRE TOUR: DAYS FOUR AND FIVE

Chenonceaux to Chambord

(45 miles)

- Go left on the D41 outside the Chenonceaux château for 1½ miles.
- In Civray de Touraine, turn right on D81 (sign: Amboise) and ride for a little over 6 miles.

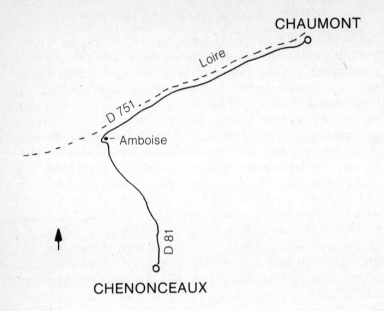

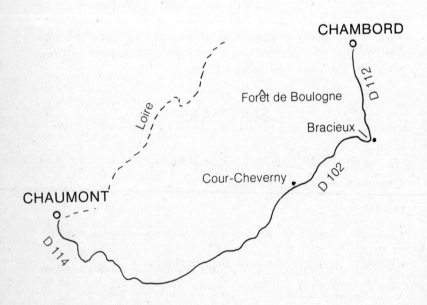

- Turn left at the next intersection (sign: Amboise).
- Follow the signs to Amboise Centre and sightsee.
- Continue on the quai General-de-Gaulle, the D751, for approximately 9 miles into Chaumont for lunch.
- Take the D114 uphill with the Chaumont château to your right for about 2 miles.
- Turn left toward Valaire. Your turn will be just before a line of forest.
- After one mile, at a three-fork intersection, go right (sign: Sambin).
- In Sambin, turn left at the first intersection and right onto D52 at the monument to the local war dead (signs: Fougères, Bièvres).
- After 2 miles, in Fougères, take the middle fork at the intersection in front of the church (signs: Fresnes, Contres)
- After just 100 yards, go first left then right to stay on D52 for approximately 11½ miles (sign: Cour-Cheverny) into Cour-Cheverny.
- Turn right toward Bracieux (sign: Centre Ville).
- In the *centre ville*, go left on D102 (sign: Bracieux).
- Go straight at the light (signs: Bracieux, Paris) and cycle for 3½ miles.
- In Tour-en-Sologne, take D102 to the right (sign: Chambord).
- Turn right at the next intersection on D102 (sign: Bracieux) on into Bracieux following the Toutes Directions signs.
- Turn left at the sign that says Chambord and again at the sign for Blois and Chambord.
- Turn right at the next Chambord sign, crossing the Beuvron.
- Go right at the fork onto D112 (sign: Chambord) and pedal almost 5 miles straight through the forest to Chambord.

DAY SIX: CHAMBORD TO ORLÉANS

After croissants and coffee, you will be ready for a 35–40 mile jaunt to the home base of one of history's most fascinating figures, Joan of Arc. The morning's ride takes you to the wonderful, ancient town of Beaugency for lunch and exploring before cycling the back way into the outskirts of Orléans. Awaiting you is dinner with one of the region's finest chefs.

Begin today's ride by coming back into Chambord village on D33. (signs: Thoury, la Ferté St.-Cyr) You'll first ride out through open fields on a cypress-lined road with a final view of the château. The road unfolds straight through deep forests alternating with golden fields. You'll pass a very old stone wall on your left before you enter **Thoury.**

At the intersection, go straight, remaining on D33. (sign: Crouy-s.-Cosson)

When you come into **Crouy-sur-Cosson**, take a right onto D103. (sign: La Ferté St.-Cyr)

In **La Ferté St.-Cyr**, turn left on D925. (sign: Beaugency) The road becomes slightly uphill then levels out through a wooded area that opens on meadows. Follow the signs into Beaugency.

At the busy intersection with D951, go straight across staying on D925, about 3½ miles into **Beaugency.**

At the T intersection, turn left and cross the famous arched bridge over the Loire River. Follow the signs into the *centre ville* for lunch.

Beaugency is a pleasant town to explore, with its medieval streets, strong sense of history, and several dining possibilities. The bridge you crossed to enter the city was for centuries the only span across the Loire between Blois and Orléans. Consequently, it became the focus of power struggles among the local nobility and between the French and English. During your stop here you may want to visit the fifteenth-century Château Dunois, which contains a medieval museum of furniture, toys and costumes, and paintings and sculpture. Beaugency also houses several old churches, towers, and hospitals dating from the Middle Ages.

L'Abbaye de Beaugency (2 quai de L'Abbaye, 45190 Beaugency; tel. 38–44–67–35). This is the place for "carbo-load-ing," or a long, leisurely lunch of regional game or fish. Its terrace overlooks the bridge and Loire, and the interior is richly decorated. (Moderate)

Hostellerie de l'Écu de Bretagne (place du Martroi, 45190 Beaugency; tel. 38–44–67–60). This quieter, country inn is noted for its menu of classic French and regional dishes and homemade fruit pies. (Modest–Moderate)

You will also find a variety of *boulangeries* for gathering picnic supplies, and the Pizzeria du Pont, with its outdoor tables by the Loire, can provide a quick light meal before completing the afternoon's ride into Orléans.

Ride back across the bridge. At the fork, go left on D19. (sign: Lailly-en-Val)

At the next intersection, a stoplight, ride straight across on D19. (sign: Jouy-le-Potier)

Turn left on D103. (sign: Jouy-le-Potier) You'll immediately pass an old stone barn on this mostly flat road. There will be some very slight inclines on this ride into **Jouy-le-Potier**.

At the T intersection in town, go left on D15. (signs: Olivet, Orléans)

After a few hundred feet, fork right on D7. (sign: Ardon) The road remains level here except the hill to cross the autoroute.

In Ardon, veer left onto D168. (sign: Orléans) You'll enter a lushly forested area where you'll wend your way past private châteaux set back in the woods, groves of evergreens, and part of a military camp on your left.

Stay on D168, following the signs into Olivet.

At the intersection, bear right. This brings you into the town of Olivet. (sign: Orléans)

This street winds to the left then to a multiple intersection where you'll make a quick right onto rue Marie-Simon. Olivet, on the outskirts of Orléans, is a blend of the old and new France. You'll be riding through town on a series of streets that will take you to the edge of Orléans, where we discovered two magnificent hotels to rest and to serve as home base for excursions into Orléans *centre*.

Turn left on rue Hermé.

At the light, go right across the pont Mont le Clerc. At this next intersection you'll turn right or left depending on your choice of hotel.

To your right, along the river Loire is Le Plissay-Hôtel Calme (allée des Villas, 45160 Olivet; tel. 38–66–02–12). This hotel, a converted manor, is set on the riverbank, and the beautiful view is an impressionist's dream. The room rate includes breakfast, the hotel has its own pool, and the host is very pleasant. (Modest)

If you turn left after crossing the bridge, you'll fork left at the famous flowered clock and continue for several long blocks before encountering another tempting choice: Les Quatre Saisons (351 rue de la Reine-Blanche, 45160 Olivet; tel. 38–66–14–30). The three-star hotel is small, two-storied, and also set on the river. It is infused with a soft palette of light through the many flowers and heavy trees. The very popular four-star restaurant, À Madagascar (315 rue de la Reine-Blanche, 45160 Olivet; tel. 38–66–12–58), is right next door, and boat rides on the Loire are available out the front door. (Medium)

Orléans has not fully recovered from the damage wrought upon it during World War II. Joan of Arc is still the main attraction here, and if you should pass through on May 8, you may participate in the celebration of her liberation of the town.

WHERE TO STAY AND DINE IN THE CITY OF ORLÉANS

There are other attractions worth seeing in Orléans, such as the Cathedral of St. Croix (almost as large as Notre Dame) and the Musée des Beaux-Arts, but none more worth spending a few hours in than La Crémaillèrre (tel. 38–53–49–17) on rue N.-D.-de-Recouvrance. Paul Huyart is *chef de cuisine* here, and we hope he continues to be for many years. His cooking is innovative and magical. Every course tops the one before. Although you can by judicious ordering stay in the Medium range, you may be tempted as we were to take the Top off here. It is well worth it.

If La Crémaillère is full, try La Poutrière or the Auberge de la Montespan. Both are fine choices, the former more imaginative, the latter more conservative.

For lodgings, a favorite selection at this point in the tour is to splurge at the Sofitel Orléans. It is big, right downtown, with a swimming pool and all conveniences.

SUMMARY

LOIRE TOUR: DAY SIX

Chambord to Orléans

(35–40 miles)

- Come back into Chambord on D33 and remain on D33 6 miles, through Thoury, into Crouy-sur-Cosson.
- Turn right on D103 (sign: La Ferté St.-Cyr) for 3 miles.
- In La Ferté St.-Cyr, turn left on D925 for about 8½ miles into Beaugency for lunch.
- After lunch, recross the bridge and go left on D19 (sign: Lailly-en-Val).
- At the next stoplight intersection, ride straight across staying on D19 (sign: Jouy-le-Potier).
- Turn left on D103 after a little over 5 miles on D19.

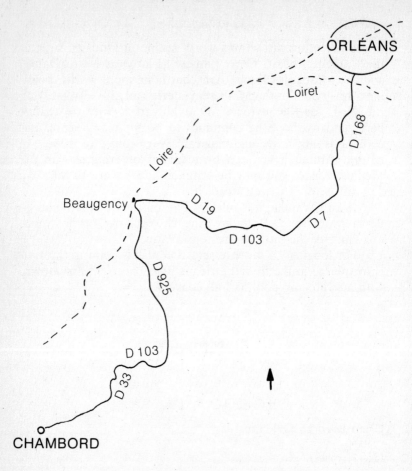

- 4 more miles take you into Jouy-le-Potier, where you go left on D15 (signs: Olivet, Orléans).
- After a few hundred feet, fork right on D7 (sign: Ardon) for 3½ miles.
- In Ardon, go left on D168 (sign: Orléans).
- Stay on D168 6 miles into Olivet.
- At the first intersection in town, bear right, which brings you into Olivet. The street winds to the left, then to a multiple intersection.

- Make a quick right onto rue Marie-Simon.
- Turn left on rue Hermé.
- At the light, go right across the pont Mont le Clerc.
- Turn right or left depending on your choice of hotel.

THE MAGNIFICENT

DORDOGNE

STUDENTS OF PREHISTORY AND DEVOTEES OF THE TRUF-
fle will feel very much at home here in this beautiful and
fertile region. You will be able to marvel at the stunning cave
art left by our ancestors, and you will have the opportunity
to savor the rich and earthy cuisine of this ancient land. All
around you will be the unspoiled charm of the countryside,
with its deeply forested landscapes of chestnut, oak, and pop-
lar, and quiet river scenes with full, swaying willows. Escarpments rise dramatically amid the rolling hills, with intriguing
châteaux commanding views of flower-carpeted meadows.
The Dordogne River is one of the most beautiful in France,
but there are many other less well-known waterways that wind
through the region. For a cyclist, the terrain is perfect. There
are country lanes everywhere to explore, and you can make
your rides as challenging as you want by staying on the flat
or charging up into the hills. The Dordogne is a feast for
every sense. As you ride along, your eyes will be inundated

with the whole range of greens, as well as the contrasts of limestone cliffs and river valleys.

The Dordogne has the incredible village of Rocamadour, which perches on a high cliff and is regarded by the French as one of their most remarkable sites. It is also one of the most visited, so plan your arrival accordingly. Some of the key cave-painting sites are now closed to the general public, because the light and the breath of thousands of visitors damaged these priceless treasures. The most famous, Lascaux, has been closed to the public since 1963. If you are a bona fide scholar you might be able to wrangle one of the rare invitations to see the paintings; otherwise you will have to settle for the excellent replica. You can still visit some originals, however, but you will need to plan your arrival at these sites carefully. Mid-July to mid-August are bad times to go to this region, as huge lines and diesel-belching buses will mar your visit. For much-visited sites such as Les Eyzies-de-Tayac you will want to go early in the morning or late in the day to avoid the crowds. Regardless of the crowds, these sites are musts, true treasures of the human family.

THE CUISINES AND WINES OF THE DORDOGNE

The centerpieces of this region's cuisine are *foie gras* and truffles. At least once in your life you should probably treat yourself to *tourte de truffles à la périgourdine*, which is a truffle and *foie gras* pie with a healthy measure of cognac in it.

Truffles and wild mushrooms of the region are used in a variety of dishes. Truffles, which grow underground, were once sniffed out by elderly virgin women. When virgins became harder to find, muzzled pigs were used to find the elusive fungus. Now dogs are used on truffle hunts, but if you are lucky you may still see a man heading out with a leashed pig to get the treasured truffle.

Potato fans should be on the lookout for a menu item

called *pommes sarladaises*, potatoes slowly cooked in goose fat, sometimes flavored with truffles. It is utterly delicious, and a specialty of the Périgord/Dordogne region. For dessert, keep your eye out for a regional specialty called *clafoutis*, a moist rich cake loaded with cherries. Two cheeses of the region bear special mention. Echourgnac, made by local monks, is rich and satisfying, while goat-cheese fanciers will appreciate Cabecou, a pungent and nutty cheese which comes in small disks about an inch-and-a-half in diameter. The fresh produce of the region is renowned for its flavor and the local chefs' ingenious manners of preparation.

You will be next door to one of the great wine regions in the world, Bordeaux, home of vigorous reds and whites of many styles. If you wish to taste the wines of the immediate neighborhood, those from Bergerac and Cahors are considered among the best. For an aperitif, be on the lookout for the Fénelon, made with Cahors wine flavored with berry and nut liqueurs.

PÉRIGUEUX

We begin our tour in the old capital of the Périgord region, Périgueux. After arriving in the city and walking around for a bit, you will notice that the three distinct sections of the town represent a cross-section of French history. There is an ancient Roman town known as the Cité, while on the verge of the hill stands the medieval section; the modern town lies to the west. The cathedral, located in the medieval section, is worth a visit. It is one of the largest churches in southwest France. Its domes and turrets give it an Eastern flavor; you may, if you have some spring left in your legs, climb to the roof and use it as a vantage point to survey the area. There is another church in the Roman sector, more ancient, that can also be visited. The Musée de Périgord is of interest to prehistory buffs because of its archeological relics, but there are also displays of antiquities dating from the Roman and medieval periods. The museum is closed on Tuesdays. You can also explore the ruins of the old Roman amphitheater, built in the second or third century.

WHERE TO STAY AND DINE IN PÉRIGUEUX

A pleasant modern hotel, the Hotel Bristol (37 rue Antoine-Gadaud; tel. 53-08-75-90) offers a good value and a central location. There is no formal dining here, but the breakfast is fast and fresh. (Modest–Medium)

If you would like to stay outside of town, pedal along the N21 about 5 miles to the village of Antonne-et-Trigonant. Here in this sleepy hamlet you will find L'Écluse (tel. 53-06-00-04), a big stone house lying beside a small river. This hotel is a favorite of French travelers. (high end Medium)

A fine, friendly dining experience is to be had at La Flambée (2 rue Montaigne; tel. 53-53-23-06), where the *foie gras* occupies center stage in many of their creations. If you have the fixed-price dinner you can easily stay in the Modest range, but if you are drawn to the à la carte menu you can find your way up into the Top category without strain. The restaurant has a live-lobster tank; you should try the chef's lobster and truffle creation if it is on the menu when you visit. (Modest–Top)

DAY ONE: PÉRIGUEUX TO LES EYZIES-DE-TAYAC

Our first day's ride takes us to one of the archeological wonder spots of the world, Les Eyzies-de-Tayac. The first prehistoric remains were discovered here in 1868, transforming this little market town into a major tourist destination. Keep in mind that the local museum and some of the caves are closed on Tuesdays. Early risers are rewarded with the limited tickets to the caves, which are very crowded in the summer.

Today's tour is moderate to challenging, as are many sections of the Dordogne. You will have a long ride before lunch

(24 miles), and a short (15 miles) ride in the afternoon with a visit to one of the grottoes in the area on your way into Les Eyzies.

Begin the day's ride in front of the railroad station and exit town toward Brive. Cross the bridge and continue until you see the sign to Atur.

Turn right toward Atur. Just after this turn you'll see a sign (Val-d'Atur, D2). The grade leaving the city is slightly uphill, then turns steeper and bumpy for several miles through thick woodland. You'll hook left into the town of **Atur,** a modern town which has maintained its architectural traditions by keeping its red-tiled roofs and shuttered windows.

At a T intersection in town, go straight, staying on the D2. (signs: La Cropte, St.-Alvère) You will now lose the precious altitude you've gained with a downhill run and two round-abouts, where you continue to stay on D2.

Follow the signs to Marseneix. The road ascends again through forest opening onto the first of many glorious views of the rolling hills of the Dordogne countryside. Here you'll see many signs directing you to farmhouses that sell foie gras. The road will alternate between sunlit fields and tree-canopied shade.

Stay on D2 all the way into La Cropte, past the old church.

Turn left on D45. (signs: Rouffignac, Thenon) After a little over a mile, D45 joins D710 for a short stretch that can be busy, but you'll ride it for less than 2 miles.

At a Y intersection, turn left on D45. (sign: Rouffignac) Don't take D45E. The open countryside of this section is dotted with the occasional red brick farmhouse.

At a T intersection, go right on D6. This takes you into the main street of **Rouffignac,** where we recommend stopping for lunch. You'll find a *charcuterie* on your left, and several *boulangeries* and *charcuteries* along this main street. There is a well-stocked grocery store on a corner across from the Café de France. A good place to eat your lunch is on the benches under the tree-canopied main square.

Continue on the D6 to a Y intersection, where you'll turn right onto the D32. (sign: Les Eyzies)

At another Y intersection continue on the D32. About a mile outside of Rouffignac there is an opportunity for wine tasting and purchasing the various specialties of the Périgord region. Just after this stop is a sign to the Grotte Préhistorique le Rouffignac.

Turn left off the D32 toward the Grotte. Along this road to the grotto (a bit over a mile) is a beautiful view of the valley and a château on the far hill. After descending a steep hill you'll find a small grotto where you can see a number of cave paintings and petroglyphs. When you have completed your visit, retrace your route back to the D32.

Continue left on D32 toward Les Eyzies. After leaving the grotto, the road begins to wind downhill, passing a stone quarry on the left and then opening to a valley on the right.

At the T intersection, go left on D32. (sign: Les Eyzies)

Continue on D32 E. (Follow the signs into Les Eyzies) D32 joins D47 along the riverbed entrance to the town. Your arrival in Les Eyzies will be heralded by a striking view of overhanging rock and grottoes on your right and the Vézère River on your left.

Take a left over the bridge into Les Eyzies-de-Tayac.

We recommend staying here overnight and for an extra morning before continuing to ride in order to visit at least some of the grottoes. A good way to begin is to visit the

Musée national de Préhistoire, which occupies a twelfth-century castle. You will see the castle towering over the town. The two buildings of the museum contain an impressive introduction to the archeological riches of this area. You'll have the opportunity to study geologic displays, exhibits of tools and paintings, and a depiction of the sequential evolution of the female form over thousands of years of prehistory.

Several caves are open to the public in and around Les Eyzies. Signs will direct you out the D47 (toward Paris) 1½ miles to the Grotte du Grand Roc (tel. 53-06-96-76), where for about $4 you can step back into nature's crystalized world of thirty thousand years ago. Grand Roc, poised high in a cliff wall above the Vézère River, is open from 9:00 A.M. to 7:00 P.M., and is least crowded in the morning.

Going farther out the D47 brings you to the Grotte des Combarelles, a well-preserved prehistoric art gallery discovered in 1901 with many pictures of animals left by our ancestors along 130 yards of cave wall. A second passage of this cave has similar drawings and also disclosed the tools and daily implements of our predecessors.

Traveling 4 miles the other direction on the D47 and then on the D48 brings you to one of the most famous prehistoric sites in the area, Cap Blanc. Here you can view fourteen-thousand-year-old animal sculptures in bas-relief. The cave is open year round, but the hours vary, so you may want to call ahead (tel. 53-59-21-74). If you have the time and interest, you could spend days exploring the smaller caves and sites of the area around Les Eyzies. Your hotel can provide you with tour possibilities and the current information about local caves.

WHERE TO STAY AND DINE IN LES EYZIES

A great place to stay and dine is Le Centenaire (Rocher de la Penne; tel. 53-06-97-18), which offers accommodation in our Medium category. Very charming and run by a friendly couple, this small hotel has a heated swimming pool and a little health club. The dining room serves terrific food, light and exquisitely prepared. They have fixed-price menus in the

Modest and Medium categories, with à la carte meals starting in the Medium range and going up. The chef does wonders with fresh fish and the local mushrooms. *Foie gras* does not play a major role in this kitchen, but we are pleased to report that he does not skimp on the truffles. (Modest–Medium)

A very popular hotel, and quite civilized in spite of its name, is the Cro-Magnon (route de Périgueux; tel. 53-06-97-06). The rooms are old-fashioned in decor and modern in conveniences. If you are ready for a gourmet feast, the *menu gastronomique* here is sumptuous and reasonably priced at just over $50 per person. The hotel is closed from the middle of October until toward the end of April. (Medium)

The hotel with the view is Les Glycines (24620 Les Eyzies-de-Tayac; tel. 53-06-97-07). Run by Henri and Christiane Mercat, this three-star hotel rests on the riverbank, which nurtures its flourishing garden park. Les Glycines dates from 1862 and has twenty-five rooms, its own bar and restaurant, pool, and an outdoor dining terrace so you can enjoy the idyllic panorama. (Medium)

SUMMARY

DORDOGNE TOUR: DAY ONE

Périgueux to Les Eyzies-de-Tayac

(35–40 miles)

- Begin this tour in front of the railroad station in Périgueux. Exit town toward Brive.
- Take a right at the sign toward Atur (D2) and ride for 3½ miles.
- In Atur, stay on D2 (signs: La Cropte, St.-Alvère).
- After almost 4 miles you'll come into Marseneix. Continue on D2.
- An additional 6⅓ miles brings you to La Cropte.
- Turn left on D45 past the old church (signs: Rouffignac, Thenon).
- After a little over a mile, D45 joins D710 for a short stretch of less than 2 miles.

- At the Y intersection, go left on D45 (sign: Rouffignac).
- After 3 miles, turn right on D6 at the T intersection.
- D6 takes you a little less than 2 miles in Rouffignac for lunch.
- After lunch continue on D6 a short distance, where you'll go right onto D32 (sign: Les Eyzies).
- D32 takes you all the way (with wine and grotto sidetrips) into Les Eyzies-de-Tayac in about 15 miles.

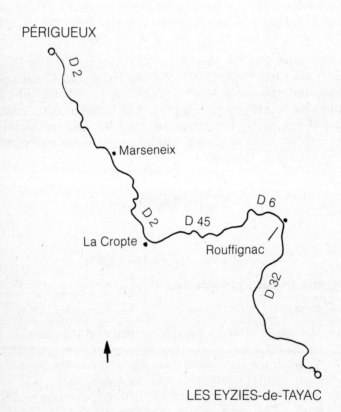

DAY TWO: LES EYZIES TO MONTIGNAC

After exploring the caves near Les Eyzies in the morning and remembering to reserve your ticket for Lascaux I or II, you have two choices for the approximately 15-mile ride to Montignac. The D65 is less traveled and offers a romanesque church in Tursac and the opportunity to view the shelters and fortress at Castel-Merle, the source of many of the artifacts displayed in area museums. The D706 affords the river panorama and possible stops at several cliffs and shelters, particularly the extensive beehive caves in the cliffs of St.-Christophe, where excavations are under way to uncover more history. Both routes are winding and will give your legs a moderate workout. The D706 (with a shortcut on the D66) passes through St.-Léon, one of the famous French villages where the intensity and variety of foliage will dazzle you. St.-Léon has many sights to tempt you from your final destination, including one of the best examples of a romanesque church and two castles to wander through.

Whatever your cycling choice, we predict you won't wander into Montignac until late afternoon or early evening, so plan your visit to the Lascaux caves early the next morning.

WHERE TO STAY AND DINE IN MONTIGNAC

There are two excellent choices for both lodging and meals. The Château de Puy Robert (route 65, Montignac; tel. 53-51-92-13) offers a great view of the river and the prehistoric sites. Beautifully furnished rooms and a terrific dining room are well worth the high price range in this hotel. Located a couple of miles out of town, the château also has a tiny heated swimming pool to help take today's long ride out of your legs. (Top)

On a lower budget one trip, we stayed at Soleil d'Or (14 rue du 4-Septembre; tel. 53-51-80-22). In the high season the rooms are let only with dinner included, but for a very reasonable price of about $50 per person. The restaurant serves a traditional version of the region's cuisine, with plenty of *foie gras* and truffles in evidence. (Modest)

VISITING LASCAUX

Since its discovery by village boys looking for a lost dog in 1940, this "Sistine Chapel of prehistory" has drawn millions of visitors. In fact, the authorities have closed off the actual paintings to the general public; now only scholars can see the real thing. But the replica, Lascaux II, displays about one hundred examples of what the paintings look like. Admission is approximately $5; it's closed Mondays and from early January until the first week of February.

Hold on to your ticket from Lascaux II and you will be admitted to the museum of cave art at Le Thot, a little over 4 miles up the road on the D706. Near the original cave there is a road that leads to another site, Regourdou, a short ride of half a mile through the woods. There is something quite wonderful about sitting down for a picnic on a spot where your ancestors sat twenty thousand years before.

SUMMARY

DORDOGNE TOUR: DAY TWO

Les Eyzies to Montignac

(15 miles)

Two possible route choices

Route One

The D65 is less traveled and offers a Romanesque church and the buildings at Castel-Merle.

Route Two

The D706 affords the river view and possible sightseeing at several cliffs and shelters, particularly St. Christophe.

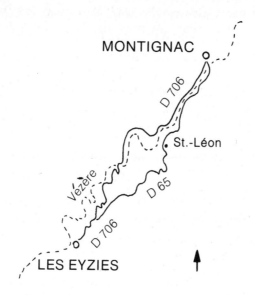

DAY THREE: LES EYZIES TO SARLAT-LA-CANÉDA

Begin today's ride by retracing your route to Les Eyzies on the way to Sarlat. Or you may want to purposely do what we inadvertently did on one tour where we misread the day's instructions and ended up lost on a *C* road. If you strike out on the back roads from Montignac to Sarlat you may experience the *real* countryside of France, where friends sit under the shade trees and interrupt their chatting to wave as you go by. We just kept consulting our map and engaging in mimed conversations with locals (*"Où est le route de Sarlat, s'il vous plaît?"*) until we arrived, weary but triumphant, at the right hotel in the right city.

This afternoon's ride, after you return from Lascaux, is

approximately 18 miles, a moderate ride through forested hills and valleys.

Head out of Les Eyzies on the D47, then south on the D48. (sign: Meyrals) As you turn onto the D48 look left to the magnificently eroded rock faces of the cliffs. You'll roll along through forest and up a long hill.

At the Y intersection take C5. (sign: Meyrals) This section of your ride is dotted with farmhouses. You'll notice when you ride into **Meyrals** that it is a proud ancient city.

At the T intersection make two sequential left turns on the D35. You'll have a pulse-elevating hill out of Meyrals.

Take the D25. (sign: Sarlat) The valley opens out in several places here. The road is very winding and hilly, and, as always in France, you'll be rewarded, this time by village tableaus and a view for miles. Just outside Sarlat the road winds down-hill into the valley, then steeply uphill to a view of one of the most beautifully preserved medieval towns in France. You'll coast down a long hill, viewing a stone arched bridge on your left.

At the T intersection, take a left on the D46 into Sarlat. Cobblestoned and lit by lanterns, this entire village is a mu-seum unto itself. If you come into Sarlat on a Saturday you can visit the market in action on the place des Oies (place of the geese). There is also a much-visited cathedral here, as well as the lovely house, now open to the public, that belonged to Étienne de La Boetie, the great friend of Montaigne. In fact, Montaigne's famous essay on friendship was written in honor of de La Boetie. But the town itself is the main attraction, well worth a few hours of slow strolls in its magic domain.

WHERE TO STAY AND DINE IN SARLAT

For a small town, there are many fine places to sleep and eat in Sarlat. If you would like to be outside the bustle of the downtown area, consider the Hôtel La Hoirie (24200 Sarlat-la-Canéda; tel. 53-59-05-62). If you choose La Hoirie, bear right when coming into town and follow the signs. Persevere up a long hill (close to two miles) with a steep climax. This glorious vine-covered old house with a lovely garden is well worth the rigorous workout to get there. Inside you will find stone walls, big beams, and a huge fireplace. There are only fifteen rooms, so reservations are a must if you arrive in the high season. (Medium)

If you want to be in the thick of the action downtown, try the Hôtel St.-Albert et Montaigne (10 place Pasteur; tel. 53-59-35-98) close to the post office. The decor is relatively bland, but the dining room is great. Try the truffle soufflé, the stuffed cabbage, or one of many preparations of *foie gras* on the menu. (Modest)

Some other bicyclists were full of good reviews of a restaurant called Rossignol, out near the city limits, but we did not have a chance to try it out ourselves. The dining room of La Madeleine, a downtown hotel, is also a fine source of the rich specialties of the Dordogne. Wild mushrooms and truffles abound on the menu here, and the sweetbreads with morels convinced one skeptic (Gay) that this gland belonged on a plate as much as it did in the inward regions of a cow.

SUMMARY

DORDOGNE TOUR: DAY THREE

Les Eyzies to Sarlat-la-Canéda

(18 miles)

- Leave Les Eyzies on D47, then south on the D48 (sign: Meyrals).
- At the Y intersection after a little over 4 miles, take C5 (sign: Meyrals).
- Meyrals appears after ½ mile. Turn left twice on the D35 and climb for 2½ miles.

- Take the D25 (sign: Sarlat) for about 10½ miles.
- At the T intersection, go left on the D46 into Sarlat.

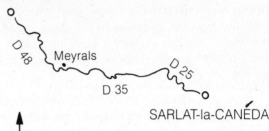

DAY FOUR: SARLAT TO ROCAMADOUR

As we mentioned earlier, Rocamadour is a major destination for tourists and well deserves to be. From a distance the houses of Rocamadour look as if they are pasted onto the side of a sheer cliff overlooking a valley. The village has been famous on and off since the twelfth century, when it became a favorite destination for religious pilgrims. If your legs are up to it, you can walk up the two hundred plus steps to the top of the village, or if you are tired out you can take an elevator for under $2. In the high season and especially at midday there is always a crowd here, so we recommend early morning and late afternoon visits to the various sites. At the top there are a basilica and seven chapels for your exploration. Check out the Chapelle Ste.-Michelle, which has stunning frescoes and walls of bare rock. The Chapelle Miraculeuse has a fourth-century clock, one of the oldest ever found. We took more pictures here than anywhere else in France, finding long vistas and new perspectives around every turn in the road.

The challenge on today's 30-mile ride will be to keep your eyes on the road. The beauty mile after mile is daunting. You'll find this area dominated by light stone houses with red tile roofs and idyllic scenery that keeps getting better.

Leave Sarlat on the D46 toward La Roque-Gageac. The road is initially busy with traffic that thins out later. Just before the beautiful village of Vitrac you'll encounter an intersection.

Turn left on D55. (sign: Vitrac Bourg) Climb a hill into the impeccably preserved village of **Vitrac.**

At the Y intersection, veer right. (signs: Monfort, Caudon)

Over the hill, turn left on D703. (sign: Souillac) With the Dordogne visible on your right you're now entering the most exceptional area of this ride. Tree-crowned peaks overshadow orchards, and wide vistas and riverbank clusters of poplars accompany you on this fairly level section of road.

Monfort Castle will appear soon on your right. You'll know you've found it because many photographers will be grouped in the field angling for the best view. This coveted site with its superb view of the valley now supports the fourth Monfort Castle, which has itself been restored. The Dordogne has been a strategic border through much of France's history, especially during the Hundred Years' War when it formed the disputed boundary between France and Britain. Don't be so struck by the castle that you overlook the stone-roofed village at its foot. As we reluctantly rode on we gazed over the stone walls for another breathtaking view of the Dordogne. The curve of the road provides another backward look at the hill and castle.

As you continue on the D703 you'll pass a twelfth-century church in **Carsac Aillac,** which you'll exit under several rock overhangs.

At the fork, stay on the D703 all the way to Souillac. This river valley is very pleasant and fertile, full of well-tended fields and rich multihued trees and bushes. In this section we were seduced and waylaid by a roadside stand for truffles.

The D703 leads into **Souillac,** where we recommend stopping for lunch. The very pretty town, built on drained marsh, has a few good inexpensive restaurants along the main street and several outdoor cafés with tables for people-watching. If you have time, visit the thirteenth-century abbey around which the town grew and thrived.

Take the D43 out of town. (direction: first toward Cahors, then through an intersection toward Rocamadour) The primarily level road here rolls right beside the Dordogne, providing a view of trees reflected in the placid water. When you come to the old bridge crossing the Dordogne, we'd recommend walking your bicycle across to avoid catching the wheels in the wide cracks.

After this bridge the road transforms into hill and vale, with a long downhill and several switchbacks.

In **Lacave** stop to visit the large and impressive caves.

Turn right onto the D247. (sign: Rocamadour) You will burn off your lunch on this very challenging 2-mile hill. After the initial thrust the slope moves uphill more gently. We found this route much less frequented by the Rocamadour pilgrims.

At the top of this climb to the back door of Rocamadour, you'll see a popular hotel. The road levels out and is lined by old, stone walls. The countryside here is more arid and hilly. You'll begin winding gently downhill, passing a tourist area perched on the hill overlooking the town, then coast through a steep downhill into **Rocamadour.**

There is hardly anything to prepare you adequately for the sight of Rocamadour. When you see the village, quite possibly shrouded in mist, impossibly perched on the side of the cliff, you will feel what it must have been like for a medieval pilgrim to reach this holy destination.

Rocamadour doesn't encourage its guests or residents to sleep late. At 8 A.M. the bells go off with a vengeance. Be advised that this is a well-visited site. We found it best to lock up our bicycles and explore the narrow roads and packed shops of town on foot.

WHERE TO STAY AND DINE IN ROCAMADOUR

One quiet little hotel that made us comfortable was Ste.-Marie (place des Senahles; tel. 65-33-63-07). This *maison* offers a small number of charming rooms and sturdy cuisine at bargain rates. (Modest)

We were in the mood for vegetarian food one night and ate in the pleasant country dining room of the Ste.-Marie. Kathlyn had a bowl of delicate vegetable soup and a plate of *pommes forestière*, which are cottage fries raised to an art by being slowly cooked in goose fat and liberally sprinkled with wild mushrooms. The chef did not skimp on the garlic. Gay had *pommes quercynoises*, which were glorified french fries with herbs, light and moist, as much like normal french fries as the Taj Mahal is like a pup tent. (Modest)

If you would like to be outside the town's high pitch of tourist energy, go out the N140 a little over 2 miles and look for the Château de Roumegouse. A fifteenth-century château, this elegant hotel served as our home base during one of our explorations of the Dordogne. There are only eleven bedrooms, so book early. Lodgings here are in the Top range and worth it, though you can dine in the Medium range in the friendly dining room. Classical Périgord cuisine is the fare here, with an emphasis on deep, richly flavored sauces and freshly caught river fish. (Medium–Top)

SUMMARY

DORDOGNE TOUR: DAY FOUR

Sarlat to Rocamadour

(30 miles)

- Exit Sarlat toward La Roque-Gageac on the D46 and pedal for 3½ miles.
- Just before Vitrac, turn left on D55 (sign: Vitrac Bourg).
- At the Y intersection, veer right (signs: Monfort, Caudon) for less than 2 miles.
- Over the hill, turn left on D703 (sign: Souillac).
- The D703 takes you through exceptional scenery for about 15 miles all the way to Souillac. Lunch stop.

- Take D43 out of town, first toward Cahors, then through an intersection toward Rocamadour.
- 6 miles of pedaling takes you into Lacave and its caves.
- Turn right onto D247 (sign: Rocamadour). The road climbs challengingly for about 2 miles, then levels out and downhill the remaining 4 miles into Rocamadour.

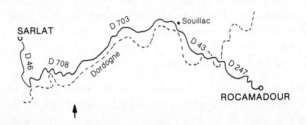

DAY FIVE: ROCAMADOUR LOOP

Now that the kinks are out of your legs, we will stretch the mileage a bit today to 40–45 miles. This alternately hilly and level loop allows you to visit some of the most famous caves of the region and what may be the prettiest village in France. If your legs and time permit, you can also take a short detour into the lovely town of St.-Céré. We suggest starting this day early.

Go back up the hill on D32. You may want to stop briefly at the top to view the small but exquisite cave of limestone dams and other formations, which also houses some twenty-five-thousand-year-old paintings.

Turn onto D673. (signs: Martel, St.-Céré) The road is gently uphill as you cross the N140 and continue on the D673. After about ½ mile you'll see a beautiful château on your left, with cows resting in front. You'll climb an exhilarating hill into the charming village of **Alvignac,** a good-sized village with several stores to stock up on supplies for the ride.

Turn left onto D20. (direction: Miers) The road then has a long downhill, then an uphill after an intersection where you remain on D20. You'll glimpse the valley from time to time through the trees.

Take a right on the little road into Miers.

Turn on D91 toward Padirac. The road here is reminiscent of English country lanes, with low, mossy stone walls enclosing rich fields. We exchanged greetings with shepherds here herding their sheep on bicycles. The fairybook road rolls up hill and down dale through small village scenes.

At the intersection with D90, turn left. (direction: Gouffre de Padirac) Follow the signs to Gouffre de Padirac. Save one and one-half to two hours to tour this famous chasm by elevator, foot, and boat. Hollowed by an underground river, this subterranean world of rivers, wells, and huge caves beneath the chasm has inspired centuries of superstition. The river opened a large passage which was discovered in 1889 and which leads to the spectacular Great Dome. Many expeditions have continued to map the web of passages and caves in this renowned site.

After your visit, take D90 toward Gintrac and Vallée de la Dordogne.

At the Y, take the left road toward Miers, which becomes D60.

Turn right on D91. (direction: Miers) You'll ride uphill past a church on your left.

Turn right on D11. (sign: Montvalent)

Stay on D11, which turns right just after the railroad tracks. (direction: Martel) The last time we rode this route we only saw a handful of cars on the back roads. You'll travel alongside stone fences with a proliferation of blackberry vines everywhere, winding downhill to the intersection.

Turn right on D43. (sign: Floriac) You may catch your breath as you enter this dazzling section of the Dordogne. You'll negotiate the narrow, ancient streets of **Floriac,** and follow the signs toward Mezels. Watch for little roadside markers that identify D43, which will assure you that you're on track.

You'll see a bridge to your left; stay right. Continue on D43 through **Mezels** and on to **Carennac,** the quintessential French village we promised you. Feast your eyes on the former home of Fénelon (where even the public toilets are charming), overlooking men fishing on the river. Parts of the village appear much as they did in the sixteenth century, with brown tile roofs, mossy walls, and clustered houses and shops around the ancient priory. We recommend wandering around and stopping for lunch here. You can choose from the Auberge du Vieux Quercy, a *crêperie*, the Hôtel Fénelon on the main road, or any café you discover in your meanderings.

Continue on D20. (direction: Vayrac)

Very shortly you'll come to an intersection and turn on D30. (sign: St.-Céré) You now enter into deep woodland, with the Dordogne to your left. After several miles the road widens out and becomes level and smoother.

At the intersection with D673, decide whether you have time and energy for a tour around St.-Céré (stay on D30 for about 1½ miles into the town) or turn right on D673. (sign: Gramat) If you detour into St.-Céré, you will see an affluent junction of ancient routes and several important current roads. St.-Céré has an old town with several sights, as well as its lovely view of the Bave Valley. From St.-Céré you have approximately a twenty-one-mile ride back to Rocamadour.

On D673, the road heads uphill, which provides a long panorama of miles of Dordogne green. The D673 is a slightly busier road, but it is sufficiently wide to feel comfortable gazing at countryside instead of watching for vehicles. Do watch for the Grotte de Presque on your left just off the road. This cave specializes in "frozen falls" of rock and named chambers of stalagmite formations, such as Red Marble Hall and the High Chamber.

A couple of miles beyond the grotto, you'll have a choice to make of whether to go see another beautiful village. If you turn right on D38 you'll come to the Autoire Amphitheater after a couple of miles, overlooking both the Autoire River and its waterfalls and the village of Autoire. You'll have the opportunity to soak up the medieval ambiance of closely clustered timber houses with the traditional brown-tiled roofs and elegantly coiffed mansions and grounds. If you choose this excursion, return on the D38 to rejoin the D673.

Follow the D673 all the way back to Rocamadour. You may find that a change in the weather and the direction from which you reenter the village give you yet another perspective on this fascinating site. Above Rocamadour on L'Hospitalet road are several restaurants with views. One with a terrace, which also houses a hotel, is the two-star Hôtel Le Belvédère (tel. 65-33-63-25). This modern accommodation is pleasant and clean, a good choice if you're looking for spacious surroundings. You can ride a little train, visit the religious relics, or just rest over your espresso and watch the weather and light sculpt the valley and village. (Modest)

SUMMARY

DORDOGNE TOUR: DAY FIVE

Rocamadour Loop

(40–45 miles)

- Leave Rocamadour back up the hill on D32.
- Turn on D673 (signs: Martel, St.-Céré) and ride 4¼ miles into Alvignac.
- Turn left on D20 (direction: Miers) about 2½ miles.
- Take a right on the small road into Miers.
- Turn on D91 toward Padirac for about 2 miles.

- At the intersection with D90, turn left and follow the signs to Gouffre de Padirac.
- After visiting, take D90 toward Gintrac and Vallée de la Dordogne.
- At the Y, take the left road toward Miers, which becomes D60.
- Turn right on D91 (direction: Miers) after about 1½ miles.
- Turn right again on D11 after less than a mile (sign: Montvalent).
- Stay on D11, which turns right just after the railroad tracks, for between 5 and 6 miles (direction: Martel).
- Turn right on D43 (sign: Floriac).
- Continue on D43 7½ miles through Floriac and Mezels and into Carennac for lunch.
- Continue on D20 (sign: Bayrac).
- Very shortly, you'll come to an intersection and turn on D30 (sign: St.-Céré) for a woodland ride of 6 miles.
- At the intersection with D673 (if you don't visit St.-Céré), turn right on D673 (sign: Gramat).
- D673 takes you the 14½ miles all the way back into Rocamadour.

DAY SIX: ROCAMADOUR TO LA ROQUE-GAGEAC

This 42-mile day carries you through several different kinds of countryside to one of the most idyllic villages in this area. Your morning will be challenging, your afternoon less so, traveling on gently sloping hills and level stretches as you return along the opposite bank of the Dordogne from a few days ago.

From L'Hospitalet road, take D673. (sign: Souillac) Be sure to admire the view before saddling up. If you start early you may have a greater chance for quiet observation. The buses begin arriving about 9 A.M.

Your ride is initially level and slightly downhill. As you start leaning into the steeper downhill, you may be grateful you are riding in this direction. The very windy road leads though arid, rugged, rocky, low brush country reminiscent of parts of Southern California. You'll enter a valley with a trout farm on the left by a lushly beautiful meadow. Over the bridge, it is your turn to climb. The grade starts up moderately about 3½ miles outside of Calès, then inclines up more sharply on the other side of the valley. After about two miles of steep climb the road inclines more moderately into **Calès.** You may want to stop for a coffee break at Le Petit Relais before continuing. You'll stay on D673. First you'll crest a hill and stay left and inside the crest of the ridge for approximately ½ mile. The road then begins to descend. In the fall you can see the heathery effect of leaves turning across the valley. You'll ride slightly uphill around the valley and then more steeply just outside **Payrac.**

Turn on N20. (sign: Cahors)

Then turn right on D141 right across from the snack bar. (sign: Lamothe-Fénelon)

You may find yourself breathing more easily as the road turns downhill in the first mile through fields and a deep forest canopy. We made a blackberry-picking stop here. The cows came over to inspect us, giving us a close look at how large and contented these French cows are. Our thoughts turned to the possibility of thick cream for the blackberries, urging us back on the road toward lunch. We recommend picking up supplies for a picnic in **Lamothe-Fénelon.**

Turn right on D12. (signs: Masclat, Souillac)

Ride straight through at the next intersection, where you may find an open *auberge du crémier* (ice cream stand) if you are in high season. The afternoon part of your ride is fairly level and winds through the south side of the river valley.

Turn left on D43. (signs: Julien, Lampon) With the river on your right you'll ride up a gentle slope into **St. Julien,** a clean, well-scrubbed, up-to-date village.

Turn on D50. (direction: St.-Mondane) In **St.-Mondane** you'll have more shopping opportunities. We were enchanted here by immaculately cultivated flower beds everywhere we looked.

You can also make a short loop following the signs to Fénelon Castle, a more militant-looking structure than Monfort, with the protection of triple thick walls and towers that guard not only the castle but the sweeping view as well. There are several things to see here, including a collection of vintage cars and a chapel.

Continue on D50. (direction: Veyrignac) The Dordogne will peek out on your right at regular intervals. There is a short steep uphill into **Veyrignac,** and a less steep climb for ½ mile after.

Turn left on D704. (signs: Gourdon, Cahors)

Turn right on D50. (sign: Cenac) Stay on D50 straight through the next intersection. You'll climb an uphill grade through deep Dordogne forest, then crest and glide downhill. A few châteaux may be visible in this area.

You can follow the signs on a very short ride to view the area you've been exploring for days from the famous promontory of **Domme,** where you can let your eyes roam from the Monfort crest to Beynac. This site has been called the "Acropolis of the Périgord," and this is an accurate description of the grandeur here. Domme also boasts several walks, very grand houses, a shopping street with specialties of the region, and, of course, some caves. If you detour, take a short return to the D50, continuing left (direction: Cenac).

Turn right on D46. (sign: Sarlat) You'll cross the Dordogne here, perhaps imagining the heavily laden boats that once traversed this important waterway.

Follow the signs as D703 leads you into the hidden valley of the village of La Roque-Gageac.

WHERE TO STAY AND DINE IN LA ROQUE-GAGEAC

You have several excellent choices within a 5-mile range, depending on your desire for quiet or company, riverfront views or country sounds.

The Hôtel Le Périgord (2450 La Roque-Gageac; tel. 53-28-36-55) is a two-star hotel in the middle of a park. It is not in La Roque itself, but a few miles down the D703 toward Vitrac. Some of the forty rooms in this rather large and elegantly appointed hotel have balconies with a view of the grounds and trees. The reputation of the dining room was supported by the capacity crowd at midweek lunch. If you desire quieter environs, this hotel is a good possibility. (Medium)

If you're yearning for river sights and sounds, La Belle Étoile (24250 Domme; tel. 53-29-51-44) is a riverfront choice. The restaurant specializes in truffle omelets and various succulent duck entrées. Both your room and dining table may overlook the river, where we saw tour boat enthusiasts and canoe paddlers enjoying the placid water and the striking juxtaposition of stone-roofed buildings against holm oak-covered cliffs. Your proximity to one of the most visited sites in the Dordogne makes this a more social hotel choice. (Modest)

Our favorite is also not in the village itself. The Hostellerie de la Guérinière (24250 Domme; tel. 53-28-22-44) is about 5 miles outside La Roque-Gageac on the D46 (direction: Cahors). This exquisite converted eighteenth-century country manor rests in a large park and overlooks the little valley and village of Domme. Individual suites decorated in period style surround a small, bright, stone courtyard. Helicopter flights are available from the hotel's own port. The cordial host and the intimate gourmet dining room added to the appeal of this memorable hotel. (Medium)

WHAT TO SEE AND DO IN THE REGION

Besides canoeing, hiking, fishing, and horseback riding, you can take advantage of being in the middle of the picturesque capital of the area. Beynac-et-Cazenac is just up the road on D703 (direction: St.-Cyprien). The castle here juts above the rock providing a view of this beautiful section of the Dordogne. Another of the contested sites which survived sieges and rebuildings, this castle has an unusual quadrilateral shape and an interesting interior. You may imagine the debates of the councils of nobles that were held here.

Returning to D703 and crossing the Dordogne at D57 will bring you to Beynac's onetime arch-rival, Castelnaud Castle. As a result of being tossed back and forth between the French and English for years, Castelnaud fell into great disrepair and is still partly in ruins. A partial rebuilding was destroyed in the Revolution. Restoration began again in the late 1960s, and currently another museum, a medieval Siege Museum, is being constructed. The great attraction, of course, is the view again, in this case, of the Céau Valley. Poplars surrounding the wide bend of the Dordogne, immaculately tended fields of tobacco, corn, and other cereals, the grouped

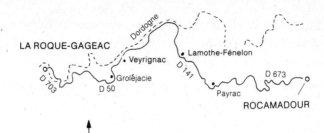

houses of Beynac, and, in the distance, La Roque and its cliffs all greet you at the top of the climb to the castle.

SUMMARY

DORDOGNE TOUR: DAY SIX

Rocamadour to La Roque-Gageac

(40–45 miles)

- Take D673 from L'Hospitalet road (sign: Souillac). This windy and very challenging road takes you approximately 8½ miles into Calès, where we recommend a refueling break.
- Continue on D673 a little over 4 miles into Payrac.
- Turn on N20 (sign: Cahors).
- Go right on D141 right across from the snack bar (sign: Lamothe-Fénelon) and cycle 3½ miles into Lamothe-Fénelon.
- Turn right on D12 (signs: Masclat, Souillac) for a little less than 3 miles to D43.
- Ride straight through at the next intersection.
- Turn left on D43 (signs: Julien, Lampon). In 3 miles you pedal into St.-Julien.
- Turn on D50 (direction: St.-Mondane) a little less than 2 miles into St.-Mondane.
- Stay on D50, riding through Veyrignac, for 5 miles.
- Go left on D704 (signs: Gourdon, Cahors) for a little over a mile.

- Turn right on D50 (sign: Cenac) and ride for 6½ miles.
- Go right on D46 (sign: Sarlat) across the Dordogne.
- Follow the signs as D703 leads you 3½ miles into the hidden valley of La Roque-Gageac.

DAY SEVEN: LA ROQUE-GAGEAC TO CAHORS

On this last day we have laid out a straightforward ride to reach Cahors in about 35 miles. The rolling hill and valley roads are moderately challenging. (*Note:* When we give you sign names, we sometimes won't include all that are listed. We include the correct ones to lead you in the right direction.)

Leave town on D703. (direction: Vitrac)

Turn right on D46. (sign: Cahors) (If you stayed at Hostellerie de la Guérinière, join the ride here.)
    The road grade is uphill for about 5 miles as you leave the heart of the Dordogne Valley. You'll continue uphill into **St.-Martial de Nabirat,** then downhill for a time. You'll pass through a succession of farming communities and may catch glimpses of châteaux in the hills. After rolling over another hill you'll descend to an intersection.

Turn right on D673. (sign: Cahors)

At the Y fork, go left on D6. (sign: Catus, Cahors) You'll ride through undulating valleys into **Dégagnac.**

Stay on D6. Passing through a slight uphill grade that turns more moderate, you'll ride through **Lavercantière** on a gently rolling road winding across a valley.

At the Y fork, turn left. (direction: Catus) Notice the mushroom symbol on the route sign.

In the center of **Catus,** turn left on D6. (sign: Cahors) This village is followed by a succession of hills and valleys. Just after a rock quarry, you'll come to a major intersection.

Turn left on D911. (sign: Cahors) The last several miles of this busy road are downhill. On your final run into Cahors, the Lot River appears on your right. Follow the main signs into **Cahors.**

Cahors retains much history from its university and commercial past as the former capital of Quercy. There are many churches, towers, museums, shops, and a cathedral to enjoy in Cahors and lovely plane tree-canopied promenades to explore. Be sure to ride or stride over the Valentré Bridge, whose medieval towers have a stone reputed to be repeatedly broken by the devil. If you had begun to wonder where the famous French wines are hiding, the southern atmosphere of Cahors is the home of a particularly famous red made from Malbec grapes and renowned for its deep color as well as its taste. Throughout the Middle Ages, Cahors wine was shipped all over Europe. At a local café you may be able to order a Fénelon, the local drink made from Cahors wine with a touch of Crème de Cassis and Crème de Noix.

WHERE TO STAY AND DINE IN CAHORS

In the center of town your best choice may be the Hôtel France (252 avenue J.-Jaurès, 46000 Cahors; tel. 65-35-16-76), a fairly large hotel in the Modest range with good services. The hotel only serves breakfast. One dining choice is La Taverne (42 Jean-Baptiste-Delpech; tel. 65-35-28-66), where many delicious regional specialties are served. The duck with wild mushrooms and several truffle dishes are especially mouth-watering, and a feast for the nose as well as the palate.

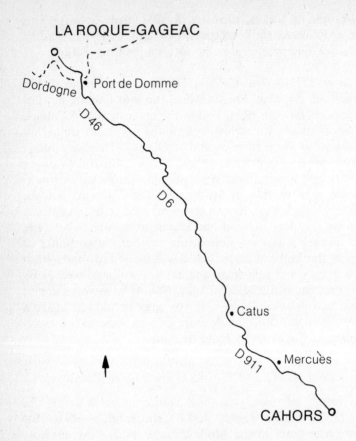

SUMMARY

DORDOGNE TOUR: DAY SEVEN

La Roque-Gageac to Cahors

(35 miles)

- Leave La Roque-Gageac on D703 (direction: Vitrac).
- Turn right on D46 (sign: Cahors) and ride 6 miles into St.-Martial de Nabirat.

- Continue on D46 for about 3½ more miles.
- Turn right on D673 (sign: Cahors).
- At the Y fork after less than a mile, go left on D6 (signs: Catus, Cahors). You'll stay on D6 for almost 20 miles.
- You'll ride through Degagnac and Lavercantière. Follow the signs to Catus on D6.
- Just after a rock quarry, you'll come to a major intersection. Turn left here on D911 (sign: Cahors).
- D911 takes you on a fast 5½-mile downhill run into Cahors on a busy road.

We don't want you to hop on your train without being aware of one last cave excursion in the area. The famous caves of Pech Merle are approximately 21 miles from Cahors. If you decide to cycle to the caves, you'll need to stay an extra day in Cahors to make a comfortable day trip. There are a couple of splendid villages near Pech Merle that you may also want to explore.

Leave Cahors on D653. (sign: Figeac) The road winds along the Lot River and through several villages.

After about 9 miles, turn right on D662. (signs: Vers St.-Géry) Stay on D662 as it follows the river.

Turn left on D41. (direction: Cabrerets)
You'll follow the serene and lovely Célé river valley for a couple of miles. When you ride into **Cabrerets** you may want to wander a bit around the beautiful setting and charming houses before following the signs to Pech Merle. There are several excellent cafés and restaurants here, as well.

Pech Merle was discovered in 1922 by two adventurous boys, after an interim of many thousands of years. The discovery has been of immense importance to prehistorians. A section of the large expanse of caves is open to the public, and includes huge caverns, drawings, and friezes of prehistoric mammals that were constructed as part of our ancestors' religious ceremonies. In your two-hour tour you can also view the justly famous "silhouettes of two horses," surrounded by strange symbols and hand prints. Part of the Amédée Lemozi

Museum is also open to the public, with displays of bones, domestic utensils and tools, other artifacts from the area, and art pieces ranging over several centuries.

Retrace your route back down the D41.

At the intersection with D662, turn **left.** (direction: Tour de Faure)

Just after **Roucayral,** turn right on D40. (direction: St.-Cirq-Lapopie) This loop will allow you the visual delight of **St.-Cirq-Lapopie,** as remarkable in its setting as Rocamadour. The village, which hovers high above the Lot River, faces an arch of white cliffs. St.-Cirq was another hotly contested site, especially during the Hundred Years' War, which has always been favored by craftsmen and artisans. The brown tile-roofed houses have been lovingly maintained and restored, often by artists attracted by the beauty of this area. Renaissance and Gothic-style windows, and ornamentations of all kinds are visible as you wander the steep, narrow roads of this popular site for visitors. Look for the church and the path to castle ruins, where the views over the village to the river and farm-land beyond are stunning. The well-equipped tourist informa-tion center has an unusual setting, the Château de La Gardette, which also houses a small museum.

Continue on the D40. (direction: Bouziès)

In **Bouziès** turn right on the bridge over the Lot River.

Turn left on D662. (direction: St.-Géry) You'll retrace your morning route now.

Just after Vers, turn left on D653. Follow this road back into Cahors for your last night in the enchanting Dordogne.

SUMMARY

Optional loop to the Caves of Pech Merle:

(approximately 42 miles)

- Leave Cahors on D653 in the direction of Figeac.
- After about 9 miles, turn right on D662 (signs: Vers, St.-Géry). Stay on D662 as it follows the river.
- Turn left on D41 (sign: Cabrerets) after about 8½ miles.
- 2½ miles takes you into Cabrerets, where you follow the signs to Pech Merle.
- Retrace your route down the D41.
- At the intersection with D662, turn left (direction: Tour de Faure).
- Just after Roucayral (2 miles), turn right on D40 (direction: St.-Cirq-Lapopie).
- Continue on D40 for just under 4 miles and visit St.-Cirq.
- In Bouziès, turn right on the bridge over the Lot River.
- Turn left on D662 (direction: St.-Géry).
- Just after Vers, turn left on D653 for the last 9 miles to Cahors.

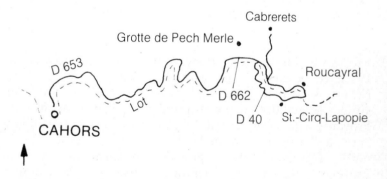

PROVENCE: VAN GOGH

AND CÉZANNE,

SUN AND WIND

ONCE WE EXPERIENCED THE LIGHT AND ENERGY OF Provence, we understood why Van Gogh, Cézanne, and Picasso were drawn to this region. The amber light of late afternoon, the raw power of the mistral winds, and the haunting feel of the old villages give this southern region a charm you will never forget. Everything looks alive and vibrant in Provence because of the saturating quality of the sunlight here: It is the most beautifully illuminated place we have ever visited. In addition to the gorgeous light, nature has blessed Provence with a mild climate. Summer lasts a long time down here, and winter is much kinder than in the chilly, damp north. The only weather problem you may encounter in Provence is the mistral, which can last from three days to over a week at times. A raw wind that roars in from the north, the mistral can play havoc with a cyclist's plans. We have arranged our tour to put the mistral at your back most of the time, and you may never encounter it if you are not touring in spring or autumn.

About one hundred fifty years before the Christian era began, Greeks were settled in this part of the Mediterranean. Unable to cope with the local tribes, the Greeks asked for help from Rome. This they got, but more than they expected: Rome took over the whole province and turned it into a rich outpost. Thanks to the climate and their sturdy construction, the Roman presence is still strongly in evidence through a remarkable variety of structures.

Provence is an experience to bask in, to savor, to cherish. With a couple of exceptions, we have kept the mileage modest on this tour, because we found Provence to be the kind of place which beckoned us to dismount and admire the countryside. To stop by the road on a sun-drenched day and sit in a field of Van Gogh's sunflowers, to smell the heady lavender blanketing the hillside: these are the sensual treats of Provence, free for the taking.

THE CUISINE AND WINES OF PROVENCE

The light, healthy Mediterranean cuisine is a cyclist's dream. The Provençal menu features garlic and olive oil, along with such vegetables of the region as eggplants, peppers, and tomatoes. Everywhere you will find spicy stews of various kinds, the most famous being bouillabaisse and ratatouille. Anchovy lovers (we are not) will salivate over a popular snack of Provence, called *pan bagnat*, which is a roll stuffed with salad and that unique sea creature. Don't worry, you can get it without anchovies. Some very famous red wines come from this region: Châteauneuf-du-Pape and Côtes du Rhône are two examples. There are several well-regarded rosé wines available here, too; Tavel and Côtes de Provence hail from the area. If your taste runs to sweeter wines, the heavier Muscats such as Beaunes de Venise will please your palate.

Our tour begins in the spectacular town of Arles. It can be reached from Paris—leaving from the Gare de Lyon—usually through Marseille. If you wish, you can take the high-speed TGV train to Marseille, switching to a regular train for the trip to Arles.

ARLES

Today we enter Van Gogh country through the town that is called "the soul of Provence." It was here that Van Gogh painted the remarkable *Starry Night* and *Sunflowers*, which he couldn't sell but which recently fetched $40 million. Arles is worth a long pause; we spent two days here—plenty of time to explore some of the winding lanes of the countryside. The town itself has well-preserved Roman ruins. Arles' reputation is so great that its actual intimate dimensions come as a surprise. You can easily walk to all the major sites through the history-drenched narrow streets. Stand in the amphitheater and see how it might feel to declaim an oration in the excellent acoustics of this two-thousand-year-old treasure. If you are a fan of Roman antiquities, the best deal in town is available at the Tourist Information Center on the boulevard des Lices. Here you can buy a ticket that will allow you access to all the sites for a little over $6. The huge amphitheater, or arena, is well worth a visit, to picture twenty-five thousand citizens of the first century cheering on their favorite lion or Christian. You can stand on top and see the bright red tile roofs leading up to the Rhône and Arles spread out in several directions. Another fascinating place to visit is the Baths of Constantine, near the Rhône. Once the site of an extravagant palace, only the baths remain now.

WHERE TO STAY AND DINE IN ARLES

Arles is a bustling place, so our recommendation is to take refuge in a quiet hotel. A couple of the best hotels, including the well-regarded Jules César, are awfully noisy. The ones we recommend give you a break from the bustle while still giving you the convenience of a central location. The Hôtel d'Arlatan (26 rue de Sauvage; tel. 90-93-56-66) is built on the ruins of a Roman palace, and in fact still has a Roman-built wall. Rooms are decorated with Provençal antiques and fresh flowers. Doubles can run toward the high end of the Medium range. Even quieter is the Mas de la Chapelle (petite route de Tarascon; tel. 90-93-23-15). Round archways, arbors, and climbing vines will greet your eyes as you walk toward this lovely old hotel. Tennis courts and two swimming pools are part of the deal here, as is the quiet setting in a six-acre park. Dinner is included with the room for a little over $100 per person. If you want to splurge, try the Grand Hôtel Nord-Pinus, an elegant four-star hotel founded in the nineteenth century, which faces the open square of the place du Forum (13200 Arles-en-Provence; tel. 90-93-44-44). You will pay for and can expect all the amenities. Its restaurant, La Carrida, does some innovative things with seafood. Try their version of sea bass, flavored with vanilla and black pepper. We also recommend the sardines grilled with basil. There are several modest two-star hotels on the side streets between the *hôtel de ville* and the amphitheater. We were particularly charmed by Le Cloître (16 rue du Cloître; tel. 90-96-29-50) and Saint Trophime (16 rue de la Calade; tel. 90-96-88-38). If you want to avoid the crowds of tourists in this famous center, you may really enjoy the two-star Hôtel des Granges, 1½ miles outside Arles toward Avignon (route de Tarascon; tel. 90-96-37-21). It has simply but sumptuously furnished rooms with balconies overlooking the garden, lots of light, tennis courts and a pool, its own restaurant with regional cuisine, and it's quiet.

Arles is full of fine restaurants. Perhaps the best known is Le Vaccares (tel. 90-96-06-17). Two fixed-price menus are available in the Medium range; à la carte may carry you up into the Top zone. The chef here has a real touch with innovative seafood recipes. We found a few things we had never seen anywhere else, such as sea-devil soup. Then there are Chef Dumas's fresh-fish creations, with unusual combinations of herbs. The food is light and inspired in this elegant upper-floor restaurant.

Practically every restaurant in town can be relied upon to provide tasty examples of the region's cuisine. Try *brandade*, a mousse of cod, garlic, and cream, or a simple dinner of *aioli* (garlic mayonnaise) atop a plate of fresh Provençal vegetables. This latter dish became our staple dinner while we toured Provence. Cheese fans will find two of the local products of interest: Banon, which comes wrapped in chestnut leaves, and its nutty-flavored cousin, Picodon, are both delicious.

DAY ONE: ARLES TO ST.-RÉMY

Today's tour, while only 22 miles, is moderate to challenging. Because of the climbs and the enticing number of sightseeing stops, we have kept the mileage short on this first day. As you pack up your bicycle and arrange your maps to begin, you may notice that the air has the taste of the sea in it. A typical day will bustle in on a hot wind to arrive sunny and bright, beckoning you to the many sensuous pleasures of Provence.

Begin today by riding past the office of tourism on the boulevard des Lices.

At the intersection with two signs toward Avignon, take the left road. Follow this street to the roundabout.

Take the road toward Les Baux and St.-Rémy. (Note that the roads in Provence are not as well marked as in our other tours.) You'll ride under two overpasses and along a tree-lined street. Follow the signs to Avignon on this busy street past the sports center on your left.

At this roundabout turn right onto D17. (signs: Fontvieille, Les Baux) A promenade of carefully tended plane trees leads you into open countryside on a slight uphill grade. You'll pass the ruins of the Abbey of Montmajour on your right. You'll view a countryside of low shrubs in sandy soil, reminiscent of parts of the Monterey peninsula. A couple of miles out of town there is a turnoff to the right on D82 where you can see the old Roman aqueducts.

As you come into Fontvieille take a right toward *centre ville*.

Take D17a, which winds through town and comes out and into D17. (sign: Les Baux) There is a profusion of unusual bauxite rock formations on your left.

Turn left on D78F. (directions: Les Baux) You'll begin to climb through an olive grove on your right, passing through slight up and down grades. After about a mile the road climbs in steep hairpin curves into **Les Baux.**

You'll see a place along the right side of the road to park your bike as you head on foot into this very popular site. After the relative quiet and easy access to sights in the Dordogne, the swarms of tourists were initially startling to us when we toured here in September.

Les Baux has a rich and unusual history. Its proud isolation is still tangible, and you can easily imagine why this perch was coveted through centuries. The white rock from which Les Baux was carved gave its name to bauxite. Once a romantic court where nobles and their ladies would debate the fine points of chivalrous love, its carved and winding streets housed lords who traced their lineage back to Balthazar, one of the Magi. Richelieu destroyed this town in 1632, angry at local rebellions against Louis XIII. It has never quite recovered; the castle is in ruins, as are many of the mansions in the environs. Still, Les Baux has a lonely charm, perched on a plateau and affording, in Richelieu's words, a "nesting place for eagles." It is also a very popular nesting place for tourists. If possible, avoid Les Baux on weekends.

You'll stretch your legs climbing through the streets of Les Baux, where you can visit museums and chapels as well as the regional offerings of the shops. Be sure to look up and out as you wander; you'll be rewarded with uniquely carved doors, hanging ironwork, and intricately decorated walls and windows.

WHERE TO DINE IN LES BAUX

We are in the neighborhood of a very famous inn, L'Oustau de Beaumanière (Les Baux; tel. 90-54-33-07), which has been called the finest country restaurant in France. Should you desire a major splurge, here is the place to do it. The inn is really a collection of four separate houses around a swimming pool and lovely gardens. A double here will definitely be expensive (perhaps as much as $400), but dinner is included, and what a dinner it will be! From the lobster soufflé to the final flambée, everything is likely to be perfect. Many people come here for the dining alone, and if you do so the à la carte menu will probably be upwards of $200 for two. (Top)

You will find the Hostellerie de la Reine-Jeanne on your right as you walk into Les Baux. This two-star hotel is a very good place to have lunch (tel. 90-54-32-06). You can select from *escargots* in garlic, pastry with *beignets* of squid, good salmon and an assortment of simple desserts, which you may consume sitting on their pleasant terrace admiring the view. (Modest)

There are several cafés and specialty shops where you can have a lighter snack. Available everywhere is the scrumptious *pan bagnat*, a round of bread covered with Provençal tomatoes bursting with flavor, egg, tuna, olive oil, and vinegar. A hands-on salad and perfect light lunch.

Leave Les Baux downhill on D27A. (sign: St.-Rémy) Your turn is right across from a postlunch wine-tasting opportunity (and golf course). The rolling hills are an odd mixture of desert landscape, olive trees, and harsh rock promontories in the distance.

Turn left at the junction with D5. (sign: St.-Rémy) The uphill grade of this section is definitely challenging, steep and winding for about a mile. It levels out into a great view of firs nestled among the rock of the Alpilles mountain chain before winding down into St.-Rémy. You'll pass and may want to stop and tour the Roman ruins of Glanum, just outside of

St.-Rémy. Built over a sacred spring, these excavations of the ancient town contain a forum, a second century B.C. house, baths, and temples. If you continue on around the cloister walls you'll find more Roman ruins with a pastoral tone. The D5 will take you on into **St.-Rémy,** the birthplace of Nostradamus and home to Vincent Van Gogh during the unhappy but wildly creative days after he cut off his ear. You can visit the Monastery of St.-Paul-de-Mausole, outside town on D5 toward Les Baux, where he committed himself. It is still a mental hospital, and though you cannot visit Van Gogh's room, you can walk the grounds and see the architecture that appears in his paintings.

WHERE TO STAY AND DINE IN ST.-RÉMY

We have chosen two excellent hotels slightly outside the center of town, where you can bask in the sun, quiet, and peace of this unassuming and deeply appealing region.

You can find the two-star Hôtel Canto Cigalo by following the signs to your right as you enter town (13533 St.-Rémy-de-Provence Cedex; tel. 90-92-14-28). The road is level initially then turns up and left for about ¼ mile. The manager assured us that its twenty fully equipped rooms need to be reserved well in advance. As you see the gardens, cool tile and warm wood, you'll be glad you made early arrangements. The Canto Cigalo offers breakfast but does not have a restaurant. (Modest)

Hidden near the Canto Cigalo is the elegantly imposing, four-star Hostellerie du Vallon de Valrugues, where you can spread out in splendor in one of thirty-four rooms. You can have the valet park your bike as you register at this establishment (13210 St.-Rémy-de-Provence; tel. 90-92-04-40). To tempt you the proprietors, M. and Mme. Gallon, offer golf, tennis, swimming, lovely grounds, and amenities by the score. The restaurant is quite famous for its regional cuisine. (Medium–Top)

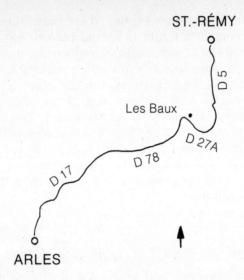

If you prefer to wander into town to dine, the little villa which houses Le Jardin de Frédéric is a tempting destination. Try the onion tart here, or one of the fresh fish specialties. We enjoyed just sitting in the town square drinking coffee and soaking up the sun and enjoying the restful pace of life. You will find sights and shops in your walking time, and you may be overcome, as we were, by the call to stillness of this wonderful spot.

SUMMARY

PROVENCE TOUR: DAY ONE

Arles to St.-Rémy

(20 miles)

- Begin the tour riding past the office of tourism on the boulevard des Lices.
- At the intersection with two signs to Avignon, take the left road.

- At the roundabout, turn on the road toward Les Baux and St.-Rémy.
- After two overpasses and a sports center, turn right at the roundabout onto D17 (signs: Fontvieille, Les Baux).
- A little over 2 miles is Fontvieille, where you take a right toward the *centre ville*.
- Turn on D17a, which winds through town and comes out into D17 (sign: Les Baux).
- After about 1½ miles, turn left on D78f (sign: Les Baux).
- The road climbs in steep switchbacks for over 4 miles to Les Baux, where sightseeing and lunch are recommended.
- Exit Les Baux downhill for 1½ miles on D27A.
- Turn left at the junction with D5 (sign: St.-Rémy).
- D5 takes you the almost 6 miles into St.-Rémy.

DAY TWO: ST.-RÉMY TO AVIGNON

This 30-mile day takes you through moderate and challenging terrain to the bustling historical richness of Avignon, built along the left bank of the Rhône. While you are getting your bearings you can taste a variety of snacks available from street vendors in the old city. Avignon was an important town even in Roman times, but it reached its full flower in the fourteenth century when the Papacy was moved there in what has come to be called "the Babylonian captivity." Popes knew how to live even back then, and the sumptuous Palais des Papes is still the number-one attraction of Avignon. During the reign of the seven popes who ruled from Avignon, art and music reached a peak along with vice and corruption. Nearby is the Cathedral of Notre-Dame, which houses one of France's most treasured works of art, the fourteenth-century Virgin of Ivory.

You'll begin today with a series of three quick junctions from the center of St.-Rémy. There is no convenient lunch stop on today's route, so we suggest packing some of your favorite fuel from the shops in St.-Rémy before leaving.

In the middle of town turn left at the Autres Directions sign.

At the next opportunity, also turn left, and stay in the right-hand lane.

Turn right onto D5. (sign: Maillane) Follow the roundabout and right fork to stay on D5. Orchards and fields will take you about four miles into **Maillane.**

Turn left at the junction. (sign: Centre Ville)

Turn right on D5. (sign: Graveson)

At the next junction, turn left to follow D5. (sign: Graveson) Leave Maillane through a glorious tree-lined street that is a virtual arboretum of Provençal trees.

Turn left at the roundabout onto D28. (sign: Rognosnas) Stay on D28 until the next roundabout.

Turn left on N570. You'll ride through more magnificent trees for about two miles.

Veer right at the Y fork.

Turn left and follow the road up over the N570. You'll be on D81. (sign: Abbaye de Frigolet) The road climbs steadily here through craggy rock formations dotted with pines, cypress and olive trees, and challenging switchbacks. Your senses may be seduced by the fragrances of thyme and lavender and the unique whisper of wind through trees. As you near the crest of the hill the Abbey of St. Michel-de-Frigolet is on your left.

    This tenth-century abbey was founded by monks from Montmajour who desired an arid, swamp-free climate. Over the centuries the abbey has been besieged a couple of times and served as a concentration camp and a boarding school, as well as housing monks. The abbey is currently open to visitors and is especially known for the quiet simplicity of its services. The grounds are an ideal place to picnic.

At the Y fork go straight. (sign: Avignon) This section of road winds downhill through deep and aromatic fir forest. As you come into **Barbentane** don't miss the windmill at the crest to your right. Barbentane also houses a seventeenth-century château rich with Italian-inspired decorations, vaulting marble terraces and formal gardens, and memorabilia of the late marquis.

Turn left on D35. (sign: Tarascon) Barbentane will be visible to your left and pear orchards to your right as you enter the fertile Rhône valley agricultural center.

Cross the Rhône on D402.

Turn right on D2. (sign: Avignon) Follow the signs into Avignon. You'll climb slightly to view the Rhône on your right.

After passing under the railroad tracks, go under the freeway bridge A9. (Ignore the first sign to Avignon.)

Take the second left up and over the Rhône. (sign: Toutes Directions)

Follow the Centre Ville signs. We advise patience getting in and out of this city. The peripheral streets of the town walls, with its eight gates and thirty-nine towers, are especially busy and the signs sometimes difficult to interpret. Avignon houses many monuments and historical buildings, and is also a cultural and industrial center of the region, which explains much of the bustle.

WHERE TO STAY AND DINE IN AVIGNON

Avignon has a wide variety of places to stay and excellent restaurants. If you would like to be in the thick of things, the modern Hôtel Cité-des-Papes (1 rue Jean-Vilar; tel. 90-86-22-45) is right at the foot of the Palais des Papes. (Medium)

If you want to have a sumptuous splurge, stay at the Hôtel d'Europe (12 place Grillon; tel. 90-82-66-92), which has been in operation since the late eighteenth century. You will sleep surrounded by beautiful antiques and tapestries. The restaurant here is also famous in the region. (lodgings Top, dinner Medium–Top)

If you want to splurge *and* be out of the bustle, we can recommend Auberge de Novès (in Noves, 8 miles out the D28; tel. 90-94-19-21). At this beautiful country estate a double with sun terrace can be over $200, but you will be well taken care of. The dining room here is a gem, drawing gastronomes from all over the region. If this twenty-two-room villa attracts you, call months in advance for a reservation. (Top, or more)

Quite possibly the best restaurant in town is Auberge de France (28 place Horloge; tel. 90-82-58-86), near the Palais des Papes. It is worth fasting all day to try the pièce de résistance here: pork, leg of lamb, and truffles in one glorious dish. Follow it with Chef Primo's dessert masterpiece, a charlotte with nuts and honey. Another famous restaurant is Hiély (5 rue de la République; tel. 90-86-17-07), with a pièce de résistance also featuring the Provençal lamb and a selection of luscious desserts, which we looked at but were too full to sample.

Two famous sites near Avignon may be worth a day trip and two nights' stay in Avignon. The Pont du Gard is a two-thousand-year-old aqueduct that is still structurally sound and quite beautiful. You can imagine how much the Romans valued water for their baths, fountains, and drinking to build this large span to carry water from Uzes to Nîmes. You can ride to Pont du Gard by taking the N100 toward Ramoulins, then left on the D981.

If you are a wine lover, you can visit the home of one of the most famous Rhône wines, Châteauneuf-du-Pape. In addition to the vineyards and the sweeping view from the ruins of the Popes' Castle, a winegrower's museum is also open for touring. You can reach Châteauneuf-du-Pape by riding

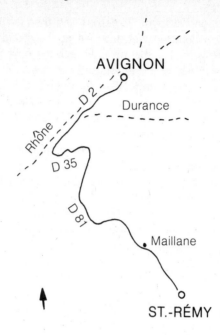

out of Avignon about 12 miles on the D225 toward Carpentras, turning left on N7, which intersects with the D17.

SUMMARY

PROVENCE TOUR: DAY TWO

St.-Rémy to Avignon

(30 miles)

- From the middle of St.-Rémy, turn left at the Autres Directions sign.
- At your next opportunity, also turn left, and stay in the righthand lane.
- Go right on D5 (sign: Maillane).
- Stay on D5 a little over 4 miles into Maillane.
- Turn left at the next possible junction (sign: Centre Ville).

- Turn right on D5 (sign: Graveson), and then left to stay on D5.
- After a few hundred feet, turn left at the roundabout onto D28 (sign: Rognosnas). Stay on D28 until the next roundabout.
- Go left on N570 and ride for about 2 miles.
- Veer right at the Y fork, then turn left and follow the road up over the N570 (you'll be on D81; sign: Abbaye de Frigolet).
- The road climbs for a little under 2 miles to the Abbey, where a picnic is recommended.
- At the Y fork, go straight (sign: Avignon) and ride over 3 miles downhill into Barbentane.
- Turn left on D35 (sign: Tarascon) and cycle for 1½ miles.
- Cross the Rhône on D402.
- Turn right on D2 (sign: Avignon) and follow it for about 6 miles.
- Ignore the first sign into Avignon. Take the second left, Toutes Directions sign, up and over the Rhône.
- Follow the Centre Ville signs into Avignon.

DAY THREE: AVIGNON TO SALON

This 40–45-mile day takes you from the bustle of Avignon through back roads and small villages to the olive center of France. The easy to moderate route first threads through the outskirts of Avignon, where the road signs are sometimes confusing, so be patient with this adventure as you head for the country.

Locate the railroad station and follow the walls of the old city south.

Turn right at the sign to Tarascon et Beaucaire.

Turn left on Moulin de Notre-Dame.

Turn right at the light, which leads to a big intersection.

Turn left. (sign: Châteaurenard) You'll be on N570. Ride across the bridge.

Just over the bridge turn left on D571. (sign: Châteaurenard) This level, tree-lined street takes you through some of the suburbs of Avignon.

Turn right on D34. (sign: Eyragues) This next section takes you through a series of junctions to keep you on D34.

Go through the roundabout toward Eyragues.

At the next junction stay on D34.

At the Y fork stay right.

Turn left following signs to the *centre ville* of Eyragues.

Turn right on D29. (sign: Verquières) You now enter gorgeous country with a gentle uphill grade that levels out to view the valley. The next part of the ride moves through a mosaic of orchards and agricultural land that is the breadbasket of France.

At a stop sign junction with D30, go straight.

At the next stop sign, turn right. (sign: Paluds de Noves) Ride on this fairly straight road into **Les Paluds de Noves** and through it on the main road.

At the intersection with D39A, go straight across. You'll pass through apple orchards on this small road.

At the T intersection, turn left. (no sign here) After about a mile on what is D31 you'll come into **Mollégès**.

Turn right on D24. (sign: Eygalières) You'll see a sign as you leave Mollégès that says Route de Jean Moulin. After approximately ½ mile, cross the D99, but go straight on D74 (route de Jean Moulin). The road climbs somewhat into **Eygalières**.

In Eygalières turn left (toward Mouriès). Stop for lunch in this pleasant village at the Chez Bebert or gather picnic goodies at the *boulangerie* up the street. If you'd like to explore this former neolithic settlement, you can walk to St.-Sixte Chapel and climb to the top of the village to scan the Durance Valley, the La Caume Mountains, and the Alpilles chain.

Down the block, turn right. (direction: Mouriès) You'll know you're on the right road if you see a sign that says D24b in a few hundred feet.

Turn left at the T intersection onto D25. (sign: Aureille) You'll ride through fragrant forest country on an uphill climb for about ½ mile.

Stay on D25 toward Eyguières and Aureille. The uphill grade here is moderate (some may say challenging).

After a long uphill, take D25a. (sign: Aureille) After another mile the hill crests and levels out. Continue into **Aureille.**

Turn left on D25b. (sign: Salon)

After ½ mile, turn left on D17. (sign: Salon) As you ride through **Eyguières** you'll be shaded by a boulevard of beautiful trees. You may see some of Eyguières' many fountains.

Continue on D17 all the way into Salon. (Watch out that you don't stray onto D569. If you get diverted, turn around and look for D17e. The turn onto D17 says Lamanon and Salon.) As you approach Salon the D17 gets busy, but we've found that other roads are even busier.

Follow the Centre Ville signs into Salon. Salon-de-Provence has recently become famous for its July jazz festival in addition to its olives and fine regional produce. You can also visit the home and small museum where Nostradamus spent his last years. The Emperi Museum, located within the medieval Emperi Castle, follows the history of the French army from

Louis XIV to World War I, and its many rooms house thousands of military items. There are several other churches and sites for a late afternoon or morning tour.

WHERE TO STAY AND DINE IN SALON-DE-PROVENCE

The consensus is strongly in favor of L'Abbaye de Sainte-Croix, a converted, spectacular twelfth-century abbey that houses twenty-two lovely rooms decorated in comfortable, country style. This hotel and restaurant is located about three miles outside Salon (take the D16) (route du Val-de-Cuech; tel. 90-56-24-55). Refresh yourself in the pool before sampling the best of light Provençal cuisine: fish and snails with fresh herbs and other imaginative creations from vegetables to sausage. (Medium)

Another exquisite restaurant can be found in Salon at 1 boulevard G.-Clemenceau: the Francis Robin (tel. 90-56-06-53), where reservations will guarantee you a choice of fine fish and lobster, delicate purées, and light pastries.

SUMMARY

PROVENCE TOUR: DAY THREE

Avignon to Salon

(40–45 miles)

- Start riding south along the walls of the old city from the railroad station.
- Turn right at the sign to Tarascon et Beaucaire.
- Go left on Moulin de Notre-Dame.
- Turn right at the light, which leads to a big intersection, where you go left on N570 (sign: Châteaurenard).
- Just over the bridge turn left on D571 (sign: Châteaurenard). This section should have taken about 2½ miles.
- Turn right on D34 (sign: Eyragues). The next directions keep you on D34 for the 6 miles into Eyragues.

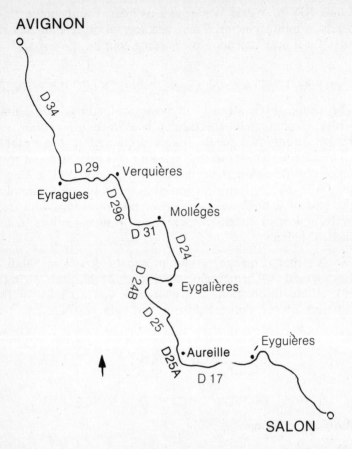

AVIGNON

D 34

D 29 Verquières

Eyragues

D 296

Mollégès

D 31

D 24

D 24B

Eygalières

D 25

Eyguières

D25A •Aureille

D 17

SALON

- Go through the roundabout toward Eyragues.
- At the next juncture stay on D34.
- At the Y fork stay right. Follow the signs to the *centre ville* of Eyragues.
- Turn right on D29 (sign: Verquières) and ride for 3 miles through the following directions.
- At a stop sign junction with D30, go straight.
- At the next stop sign, turn right (sign: Paluds de Noves). Ride through the town and straight across the intersection with D39A.
- At the T intersection, turn left.

- After about a mile on what is D31 you'll come into Molleges.
- Turn right on D24 (sign: Eygalières).
- After about ½ mile, cross the D99, but go straight on D74 (route de Jean Moulin) about 2 miles into Eygalières.
- Turn left toward Mouriès and stop in the center of Eygalières for lunch.
- Down the block, turn right toward Mouriès, with a D24b sign shortly.
- Turn left at the T intersection onto D25. Stay on D25 toward Eyguières and Aureille for 3½ miles.
- Take D25a (sign: Aureille) for over 2½ miles into Aureille.
- Turn left on D25b (sign: Salon).
- After ½ mile, turn left on D17 for 5½ miles into Salon.

DAY FOUR: SALON TO BONNIEUX

This 35-mile day has some of the best country, views, and terrain so far on this tour. Parts of the ride are quite challenging, so we've kept the mileage low. You'll have the opportunity for castle touring, wine tasting, and monument visiting along the way. Your destination, the gracefully terraced village of Bonnieux, is perched on a promontory in Luberon that overlooks a large area of the Calavon valley.

Leave Salon on D17. (sign: Pelissane)

In **Pelissane** join D572. (direction: St.-Cannat)

At the X junction just outside Pelissane, turn on D22A. (sign: La Barben) Follow the signs to the right on a slight uphill grade to the medieval château, which you'll first see on the hill to your left. This former fortress and abbey was a private home for five hundred years. You will have a picturesque view from the château, and you can see many paintings and tapestries before stopping at the local zoo across the road.

Retrace your route along the same road.

At a monument in the middle of the road, take the right fork. (sign: Cazan) You'll ride through pleasant vineyards and streams on this small road.

At the next junction, turn left.

Very shortly, turn right on D22. (sign: Cazan) The road is slightly then more moderately uphill for a couple of miles.

At the Y junction, turn right on D22. (signs: Cazan, Caves de Château-Bas) The Caves de Château-Bas are marked by a sign on the right side of the road. If you stop here in late September, you may be treated to the intoxicating aroma of grapes being processed. The Roman temple here is contemporary with the ruins outside St.-Rémy. The delicately carved corinthian capital and fluted column are well preserved.

Continue right on D22 after your visit.

In Cazan turn right on N7 for about 100 feet.

Turn left on D22. (sign: Charleval) After a slight uphill ride you'll come out into a view of the Durance valley. In **Charleval** you'll ride over the canal and down a lovely tree-lined street.

Turn right on the busy D561.

At the roundabout, turn toward the château. You're now in **La Roque d'Antheron.**

Wind through town on D561. You'll pass the Abbey of Selvacane on your left in a forested area.

Join the larger road to your right.

Take the left fork. (sign: Cadenet)

Turn left on D543. (sign: Cadenet)

Take the right fork toward the *centre ville.* After about 2 miles you'll arrive at our lunch stop, **Cadenet.**

Turn left on D943.

Turn right into the *centre ville.* Cadenet had the best fruit center we saw in France: fresh prunes and melons, as well as large juicy grapes. We suggest packing some fruit for your afternoon climb. There is the Restaurant Crêperie on the right and a bar-grill, the Café du Commerce.

After lunch, loop around and rejoin the D943 heading right.

Take the right fork to Apt-Lourmarin. Just after you turn you'll encounter another large fruit stand on the right, in case you feel your supplies are inadequate. The road climbs through airy country. The vineyards on the hills to your left and then the valley of Luberon have a cheerful, open quality in real contrast to the loamy, deeply earthy experience of the Dordogne.

In Lourmarin stay on D943. You may wish to stop in Lourmarin to visit the château, a convergence of Renaissance, medieval, and fifteenth-century additions. You can view the mountain range, Durance Plain, and Mt. Ste.-Victoire from a platform in the turret. (signs: Bonnieux, Apt)

This 6-mile section of mountain road climbs steeply through a beautiful forest of the Luberon Range. If the winds are right, you may catch the distinctively Provençal aroma of the many aromatic plants and herbs that grow in profusion here.

Turn left on D36. (sign: Bonnieux) This turn brings even more uphill climbing through switchbacks and forest.

Stay on D36 through a final switchback into Bonnieux. Among the many charms of this hillside village are the ever-present view of the Calavon Valley and neighboring towns, the ivy-covered shops and houses along the terraced streets, and, of course, a museum, this one extolling the bakery profession.

WHERE TO STAY AND DINE IN BONNIEUX

A converted eighteenth-century manor houses the ten rooms of the Hostellerie du Prieuré, an elegant and quiet hotel (84480 Bonnieux; tel. 90-75-80-78). You can dine here in season in the rich garden. (Medium)

The convivial Hôtel César has an excellent view of the valley from the restaurant windows (84480 Bonnieux; tel. 90-75-80-18). (Modest)

Up the street from the Prieuré is a bustling restaurant with an obvious fondness for garlic: Le Fournil (tel. 90-75-83-62) serves regional cuisine (which means lots of fresh vegetables and light entrées with the king of spices, garlic, much in evidence) either indoors or on their tree-shaded patio.

SUMMARY

PROVENCE TOUR: DAY FOUR

Salon to Bonnieux

(35 miles)

- Ride from Salon on D17 (sign: Pelissane).
- After 3 miles, in Pelissane, join D572 in the direction of St.-Canat.
- At the X junction just outside Pelissane, turn on D22A (sign: La Barben). Follow the signs for just over 2 miles to the castle at La Barben.
- Then retrace your route along the same road. At a monument in the middle of the road, take the right fork (sign: Cazan) for a couple of miles.
- At the Y junction, go right on D22 (sign: Cazan, Caves de Château-Bas) for 4½ miles into Cazan.
- Turn right on N7 for about 100 feet.

- Turn left on D22 (sign: Charleval) to ride a little over 3 miles into Charleval.
- Turn right on D561 for 3 miles.
- At the roundabout, turn toward the château.
- Wind through La Roque d'Antheron on D561.
- Join the larger road to your right and take the left fork toward Cadenet.
- Turn left on D543 (sign: Cadenet).
- Take the right fork toward *centre ville*, which takes you to the lunch stop after about 2 miles. Turn left on D943 and right into *centre ville*.
- After lunch, loop around and rejoin the D943 heading right.
- Take the right fork 2½ miles to Apt-Lourmarin.
- Stay on D943 for a *steep* 6-mile climb.
- Turn left on D36 (sign: Bonnieux) for the final 2-mile climb into Bonnieux.

DAY FIVE: BONNIEUX TO AIX-EN-PROVENCE

This leisurely, moderately hilly 30-mile day will take you by a back door into the cosmopolitan center of Aix (pronounced like our letter *X*), a great walking city with many attractions.

Leave Bonnieux on D36 the same way you entered.

Just out of town, turn left. (sign: Saignon) If you want to take a loop to see the Prieuré de St. Symphoriem, take a left on D32, then a series of right turns to rejoin D943.

Turn right on D943. (sign: Lourmarin) Now you will have the luxury of flying downhill for 6 miles through the canyon.

Stay on D943. This will take you around Lourmarin. Be cautious to avoid taking a left on D56.

In Cadenet, turn right. (sign: Toutes Directions)

Turn left on D973.

Turn right on D943. (signs: Rognes, Aix-en-Provence)

At the Y fork, stay left on D943. You will pass covered cultivated fields on the right, and then cross the Durance River.

Turn right toward Rognes, then immediately left on D543. The lovely aquamarine St. Christophe reservoir appears on your right as the grade turns slightly uphill. After a bit, the road levels out and passes lush vineyards, then climbs gently and moderately into **Rognes,** site of the well-known Rognes stone and an interesting church. We suggest stopping for lunch here at one of the modest restaurants or *boulangeries*.

At the Y fork, turn left. (sign: Éguilles)

Turn left toward Le Puy.

Turn right on D14C. (sign: Puyricard) You'll have a short steep climb through vineyards and fruit-growing estates, then some hills and vales to ride through.

Turn toward the sign for Château de Blaulieu. The road climbs again steadily for about ¼ mile. The old château will appear on your right. The road turns moderate now through the pines, then downhill.

At the Y junction, stay on D14. (sign: Aix-en-Provence)

In Puyricard, at the roundabout, stay on D14. (sign: Aix-en-Provence)
   The road slopes down here through the outskirts of Aix.

At the next roundabout, turn left. (sign: Aix) Follow the series of signs leading into Aix. You'll whiz down a steep hill as you enter Aix-en-Provence. One of the hotels we recommend, the Hôtel des Thermes, is on your left as you enter the city.

Follow the signs to Centre Ville. Be cautious, especially if you arrive late in the afternoon. Aix is another of the walled cities where the peripheral circling streets are considered local raceways by some of the inhabitants.

   The first thing we noticed when we pedaled into Aix-en-Provence was the beauty of the main street, one of the loveliest thoroughfares we have seen on the continent. Called the cours Mirabeau, after the great statesman of the Revolution, the tree-shaded street, with its cafés and sandstone hotels, is a very welcome sight after a day of riding in the strong Provençal sun. In fact, this town is one of our favorite places in France. This is Cézanne country, and you may still visit the studio where he painted many of his masterpieces. He was born in this bright land, but unfortunately he was not much appreciated in the local community or in the art world of Paris until quite late in his life. In fact, he recalled that neighborhood youngsters threw rocks at him as he walked back and forth to work. He would no doubt chuckle at the fact that now there are parking lots and car repair shops named in his honor, as well as hotels and restaurants.

There are many sights and activities available in this metropolitan yet relaxed city. The tourist information center can give you maps and directions to the many churches, museums, and historical monuments which abound in the area; the local color is engaging all by itself. Out on a walk we passed street vendors, various citizens' groups lobbying for support of Amnesty International and the local library, and a group of schoolboys dressed in pseudosurgical garb whose fraternity task was to sell pieces of toilet paper to passersby.

WHERE TO STAY AND DINE IN AIX

One small hotel that we enjoyed immensely is the Hôtel des Augustins (3 rue de la Masse; tel. 42-27-28-59), formerly a twelfth-century convent. You sign in at a reception desk in a chapel and stay amid stained glass, stone walls, and vaulted ceilings. Depending on your choice of rooms, the tariff here can be very high, but the wide range of modern conveniences (color TV, minibar) and the gorgeous furnishings make it well worthwhile. Our room had a skylight both in the bedroom and in the sumptuous bathroom. The bed was deliciously firm, the staff exceedingly helpful, and the room-service breakfast prompt and delectable. See if either of the rooms with private terraces are available. (Top)

Your incoming bicycle route carried you past another of our choices, the three-star Hôtel des Thermes (2 boulevard Jean-Jaurés, 13100 Aix-en-Provence; tel. 42-26-01-18). This famous spa is nestled in a restful and well-tended park. You will have the usual city amenities (TV, direct-dial phone, minibar, etc.) plus access to the hotel's large thermal pools. After days up and down hills, your muscles may draw you to this hotel. (Medium–Top)

On the outskirts of town, the Hôtel Pullman le Pigonnet (5 avenue du Pigonnet; tel. 42-59-02-90) is housed in an elegant villa. The gardens here are exquisite, and there is a swimming pool. Outdoor dining is available in the tree-shaded courtyard, but the food does not quite match the beauty of the hotel.

Better to save your appetite for Le Clos de Violette (tel. 42-23-30-71), which sets the best table in town in every way. A gourmet destination for diners all over the region, the restaurant is not easy to find (we got lost even with careful directions from our hotel—think about taking a cab). Once seated inside the stone walls of this villa, the innovative dishes will make your mouth water. Devotees of the snail will appreciate an incredible upside-down *escargot* tart. If possible, save some room for some of the creative desserts. Here even the fixed-price meals are high. (Top)

Another expensive dining establishment is La Vendôme (tel. 42-26-01-00), where you can dine inside or outside under the trees. The one dish that stands out in our memories here is a cassoulet of crab and morels. (Top)

Aix is blessed with many fine restaurants offering both regional and international cuisine, and you may find something even better than our discoveries. If you are in the mood for something lighter, several *brasseries*, serving quick and sturdy meals, dot the town's streets. Here you will find the fish soup, served with a side of "*aioli*" (garlic mayonnaise) for which the region is famous. We were last in Aix at the peak of harvest season, so wonderfully fresh vegetables abounded everywhere.

Here at the end of the tour, after all your riding, you may be ready for a little bull. In Provence you may see signs advertising *taureaux piscine*, which translates as something like "bull-in-a-swimming-pool." It is an indigenous sport to this region, and involves daring young men attempting to get into a portable swimming pool at the same time as a bull. Apparently, if you occupy the pool at the same time as the bull you get a prize. We passed up the opportunity to witness this thrilling sport, so our report is based entirely on hearsay. Provence is also home to a French form of bullfighting, which has different rules and less macho bloodletting than its Spanish counterpart.

SUMMARY

PROVENCE TOUR: DAY FIVE

Bonnieux to Aix-en-Provence

(30 miles)

- Depart from Bonnieux along the same route as your entrance, the D36.
- Just outside town, turn left (sign: Saignon).
- Turn right on D943 (sign: Lourmarin) to breeze down those 6 miles. Stay on D943 the additional 1½ miles to Cadenet.
- Turn right at the Toutes Directions sign in Cadenet.
- Turn left on D973.
- Turn right on D943 (signs: Rognes, Aix)
- At the Y fork, stay left on D943 for two miles, crossing the Durance River.
- Go right toward Rognes, then immediately left on D543 to ride 3½ miles to Rognes for lunch.
- At the Y fork, turn left toward Equilles.
- Go left toward Le Puy.
- Turn right on D14c (sign: Puyricard) and ride 5½ miles, staying on D14 (sign: Aix).
- In Puyricard, at the roundabout, stay on D14 (sign: Aix).
- At the next roundabout, turn left (sign: Aix). Follow a series of signs leading to Aix and Centre Ville.

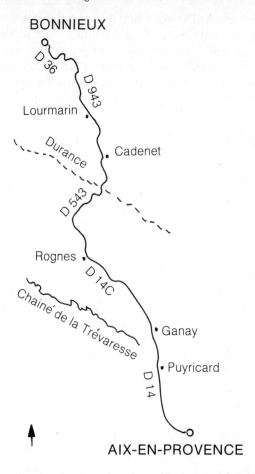

A CHALLENGING DAY LOOP
THROUGH CÉZANNE COUNTRY

We recommend staying at least two days in Aix-en-Provence, so that you can immerse yourself in the wonders of the countryside. We have devised a one-day loop of about 40 miles for those who want to ride through the colors that Cézanne celebrated. The loop circumscribes Mt. Ste.-Victoire, a limestone range of rugged peaks and canyons with deep forest and cultivated areas. Do your best to time this route for a week-day. We last did this loop on a Friday and had very little car traffic. We did, however, see and pass many cyclists testing their mettle on this very challenging ride. Pack lots of carbo-hydrates and water for this ride. Many sections of the road lack any sign of civilization (such as cafés and bike shops).

Leave Aix on the D10. (sign: Vauvenargues)

Go through the stop light intersection. (signs: Vauvenargues, St.-Marc) The steady uphill will bring you to signs for St.-Marc and the Bimont Dam, where you can turn right to enjoy the excellent wooded site of the large vaulted dam that spans the Infernet River. Afterward, the main road turns downhill and levels out into the valley.

Take the right fork at the Y intersection on D10 to go through Vauvenargues. As you come into Vauvenargues, look for the château on the hill behind the village. This seventeenth-century castle belonged to Picasso; it was his home in the latter part of his life and is his burial site now. There is no admittance to the public. This is your last opportunity for many miles to stop at one of the pleasant cafés. If you feel like stretching your legs further, you might enjoy walking to the peak of one of the nearby mountains; several hiking trails leave from the village.

Rejoin the main road and continue to your right.

Take the right fork at this Y intersection. (sign: Rians) You'll now enter a lushly forested area on a steep upgrade through the Infernet Gorges, with switchbacks and continual eleva-tion. This is your biggest climb of the day, first passing the Col de Claps then the Portes Pass before turning downhill into deep backcountry and miles of oak forest. We suggest a lunch break to celebrate the summit. The road toward Rians turns into D223, but there is no intersection.

Turn right on D23. (sign: Pourrières) This exhilarating down-hill run races through shrub-covered rock radiating the sun, then levels out into the village of **Pourrières.**

Follow the signs to Aix into town. The *centre ville* is a steep uphill climb. The town apparently earned its name, which translates as "rottenness," from the aftermath of a battle be-tween the Romans and the Celts over a hundred years before the birth of Christ, when a large number of bodies was left to rot.

Turn on D623. (sign: Puyloubier) You come into a cultivated grape-growing region here, with the mountains visible in the distance.

At the X intersection, go straight. In **Puyloubier,** on D57b, there is a bar restaurant to refresh yourself before the last homeward stretch.

Leave Puyloubier on D57 for 100 feet, then turn right on D17. (sign: Aix) The D17 will carry you all the way into Aix. One of the things your eye may catch and enjoy in this section is the bright contrast between the deep red clay at the base of the mountains and the stark white limestone of the higher eleva-tions. The countryside here is gorgeous—pure Cézanne. The last village you pass through, Le Tholonet, has some old Roman quarries that are worth a look. From here, continue on the D17 back to Aix and a well-deserved dinner.

This loop requires quite a bit of stamina, but even if you turned back to Aix after visiting the first village, Vauve-nargues, you would still see a pretty piece of Cézanne country.

SUMMARY

PROVENCE TOUR: OPTIONAL DAY LOOP

Through Cézanne Country

(40 miles)

- Ride out of Aix on the D10 (sign: Vauvenargues) and go through the stoplight intersection in the direction of St.-Marc.
- Take the right fork at the Y intersection after a little over 7 miles on D10 to go through Vauvenargues.
- Rejoin the main road and continue to your right 2 miles.
- Take the right fork at the Y intersection (sign: Rians) and ride 6 miles through challenging territory that turns into D223 (no intersection).
- Turn right on D23 (sign: Pourrières) and ride just over 4 miles into town.
- Turn on D623 (sign: Puyloubier) and cycle 3½ miles into Puyloubier.
- Leave Puyloubier on D57 for 100 feet, then turn right on D17, which will lead you the remaining 12½ miles back to Aix.

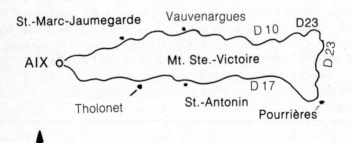

HEART OF THE WINE
COUNTRY: THROUGH
BURGUNDY AND
BEAUJOLAIS

GLORIOUS FOOD, FRIENDLY PEOPLE, AND PERFECT ROADS
for bicycling. This region was the first we ever toured in
France, and it remains one of our favorites. Here the cyclist
pedals through some of the most carefully tended real estate
in the world. In the village (sacred to wine fanciers) of Montrachet, for example, there are only nineteen acres of grapes
divided among twelve different growers. Some families make
their entire living from a few rows of the prized fruit. We
have designed this tour through villages with some of the most
famous names in the world: Pouilly, Fuissé, Gevrey-
Chambertin.

The Burgundy region has a deeply settled feel to it, and
should. Centuries ago the dukes of Burgundy were as powerful as the King of France himself. Hardly a square foot of
land has changed hands here in a long time. The main regions
we will be riding through are the heart of the Beaujolais,
the Côte de Beaune, and the Côte de Nuit, part of a larger
destination, the Côte d'Or. These areas produce wines that

are true stars of the wine world. There is a saying here: "You can't hurry the grapes." The same can be said for the Burgundians. Life moves at a slower pace, more in tune with the natural flow of the seasons. Whether you are a wine fancier or not, we predict that you will become deeply attached to this friendly land ruled by a deep concern for the good life.

On different occasions we have done this tour from top to bottom (Dijon to Villefranche) and from bottom to top. Both ways are equally satisfying, and you are welcome to take it in whichever direction suits you. Here we describe it starting in Villefranche and working our way up to Dijon. There are no bad views in this tour. Everywhere you gaze you'll see the product of centuries of loving cultivation of the natural beauties of the land. The true glories of the Beaujolais, the area of our initial rides, must be earned with some hill climbing. You'll have a strenuous workout the first three days, after which the terrain is somewhat more level. The hillsides of this area are dotted with over 180 châteaux, and you will pass many of them. Feel free to follow your intuition regarding wine sampling at the many *ventes directs*. We had some memorable experiences with the hospitable and proud owners of the vineyards.

Villefranche may be reached from Paris—leaving from the Gare de Lyon—on many trains daily, including the high-speed TGV.

DAY ONE: VILLEFRANCHE TO BELLEVILLE

Villefranche is an ideal place to start the tour, but not a very interesting town in itself. It's the commercial center of the Beaujolais wine-growing region. Our goal will be to leave town quickly in favor of the glorious heart of the Beaujolais. We recommend taking the train into Villefranche early in the day to leave time for the ride. If that doesn't fit your schedule, you can find comfortable and reasonable lodging at the Hôtel Plaisance (tel. 74-65-33-52). The tourist information office is located at 290 route de Thizy. Today's 35-mile ride is in the moderate-to-challenging range.

From the railroad station, follow the signs to Centre Ville.

Take the rue Nationale through town. This main street is just a couple of blocks from the railroad station.

Turn right at the Toutes Directions sign onto rue Victor Hugo.

Take a left at the Centre Ville sign.

Follow the Toutes Directions sign.

Go straight across at the next two lights. (sign: Cogny)

Take D84. (sign: Cogny) You'll quickly find yourself riding through small wine estates. Within a mile of town you'll find several places to sample different Beaujolais wines. Ride along the side of the hill, where we saw grapes being harvested. Blackberries are abundant here, in season.

At the next intersection, go straight on D84. (sign: Cogny) The road winds slightly up past an old wall, then stiffly up into **Cogny**. In case you have any question about whether you've arrived you'll see 15–20'-high letters written in the hedge on the hill. René Marchand wine is produced here.

Turn right on D19. This is a steep hill through town that curves around the edge of the hill and into a striking view of the Beaujolais valley.

Take a left on D504. (signs: Rivolet, Thizy)

Take the right on D19. (sign: St.-Julien) You have a short downhill break here.

At the T intersection, turn right, going uphill.

At the stop sign, go straight on D19. (sign: St.-Julien)

If you want to take the high road here, go left on D44 (sign: Montmelas). You'll continue up through vineyards and a valley view.

At the cross monument in the middle of an X intersection, go on the road that says 3+ −5. This is a steep downhill section through more beautiful country where you will probably see very little traffic.

In St.-Julien, turn on D19.

Stay left on D19. (sign: Blacé) You'll climb uphill into **Blacé,** where you'll pass a beautiful château on the left.

Go right on D19. (sign: Croix Palage)

At the next big intersection, with many choices, stay on D19. (sign: Pont Mathivet) You'll ride up hill and down dale here, then under an old viaduct.

Turn left on D19A. (sign: Arbuissonas) The road is a moderate uphill here, passing a gorgeous château on the right. A *vente direct* is available on the left as you continue through more vineyards.

At the T intersection, turn right. (direction: Cave de Clochemerle) The purpose of today's climb is to get the stupendous view of the Beaujolais, where virtually every square inch is meticulously cultivated.

Go right on D49E. (sign: Vaux en Beaujolais) The upgrade slope takes you into **Vaux en Beaujolais,** where wine tasting is available with a hearty lunch at the Auberge de Clochmerle in the Modest range. The menu includes a salmon soufflé or chicken in Beaujolais sauce. One attraction of this spot is the outdoor patio, where you can eat to the accompaniment of many bird songs. After lunch, we'll continue along the route de Beaujolais.

Turn left on D133. (sign: Le Perreon) You'll have a chance to begin digesting easily on this downhill grade. In **Le Perreon,** just past Vaux en Beaujolais, there is a bar-café, if the auberge isn't to your liking.

Turn left on D88. (sign: La Creuse) We saw as many cyclists as cars on this route, and not many of either in the first part of the ride.

In La Creuse stay on D88. The road continues uphill, with some switchbacks. We decided spontaneously to stop at the family vineyard of Michel Payen, a *vente direct.* We met his lovely wife and family for an animated wine tasting and discussion session. I rummaged for my dictionary, as did Mme. Payen, and we managed to purchase a couple of bottles of the most pleasant wine we had in the entire trip. If you stop, we'd advise saving the serious tasting for later, because the D88 becomes steeply challenging in this next forested section.

Turn right on D72. (direction: Beaujeu) Ride through dappled forest, then vineyards, as the road follows the side of the mountain and turn downhill through the little village of **Marchampt.**

Veer right through the village in a slight uphill to the intersection.

Go right on D9. (sign: St.-Vincent) The road is level and downhill here, with another great château on the left. In **Quinces,** a *patisserie* beckons the hungry.

Stay on the D9 to Belleville. We have two hotel choices for you, one in the luxurious country mode and the other more modestly appointed.

WHERE TO STAY AND DINE IN BELLEVILLE

To reach the *Auberge des Sablons,* the more modest choice, continue into Belleville.

At the stop light with signs to Macon, turn left on N6 for about a mile.

Turn right on D69. (sign: Route de St.-Jean)

Follow the signs to Auberge des Sablons.

Turn left on D109. (signs to Auberge)

Turn right on D109E. Follow the signs to the hotel, which is actually in **Taponas.** Have patience. This peaceful, clean hotel is worth the ride. The Auberge des Sablons is a two-star hotel managed by Daniele and Jean-Pierre Tardy (69220 Belleville sur Saône; tel. 74-66-34-80). They run a very pleasant and tidy establishment with fifteen rooms. The country dining room, which looks out over the garden, serves lots of fresh fish, sea bass, perch, and trout. (Modest)

The *Château de Pizay* spreads out in the middle of vineyards and is very quiet. To reach this hotel:

As you're coming into Belleville on D37, turn left on D18 (just before the bridge over the railroad tracks).

Go left again at the junction with D69. The château is immediately on your right.

The Château de Pizay (tel. 74-66-51-41) is a large converted château with a French garden in front and the forest just behind. Tennis and swimming are available, and wine is for sale here (as well as in many places around Belleville, including Henry Fessy, Pierre Ferraud, and Vins Dessalle). (Medium)

You may enjoy the fine table at the château or venture back into Belleville to experience what some call the best restaurant in the whole region. Le Beaujolais (40 rue Marechal Foch; tel. 74-66-05-31) has an interesting medieval feeling and a large selection of the regional specialties, including creamed crayfish, braised sweetbreads and kidneys, and a variety of delicious sausages. The chefs in this region delight in complex and unusual combinations. Your meal at Le Beaujolais will probably take a leisurely couple of hours. (Modest–Medium)

SUMMARY

BURGUNDY-BEAUJOLAIS TOUR: DAY ONE

Villefranche to Belleville

(35 miles)

- Start at the railroad station and follow the signs to Centre Ville.
- Ride on the rue Nationale through town.
- Turn right at the Toutes Directions sign (rue Victor Hugo).
- Go left at the Centre Ville sign.
- Follow the Toutes Directions sign.
- Go straight across at the next two lights.
- Take D84 (sign: Cogny).
- At the next intersection go straight on D84 (sign: Cogny). From Villefranche to Cogny is about 5 miles.
- Turn right on D19 and ride about 2 miles.
- Take a left on D504 (signs: Rivolet, Thizy) for a short distance.
- Turn right on D19 for over 3 miles to St.-Julien. At the cross monument in the middle of a X intersection, go on the road that says 3 + − 5.
- In St.-Julien turn and stay left on D19 (sign: Blace) less than a mile into Blace.
- Go right on D19 (sign: Croix Palage).
- At the next big intersection, stay on D19 a little over a mile.
- Turn left on D19A (sign: Arbuissonas).
- Turn right at the T intersection (direction: Cave de Clochemerle).
- Go right on D49E (sign: Vaux en Beaujolais) 4½ miles into Vaux en Beaujolais. Lunch break.
- Turn left on D133 (sign: Le Perreon) about 2½ miles into Le Perreon.
- Turn left on D88 (sign: La Creuse) and stay on D88 through La Creuse a little over 4 miles.

- Turn right on D72 (direction: Beaujeu) and ride 3½ miles, through the village of Marchampt.
- Veer right through the village to the intersection, where you turn right on D9 (sign: St.-Vincent).
- After almost 4 miles you'll come into Quinces.
- Stay on D9 the 5 miles into Belleville.

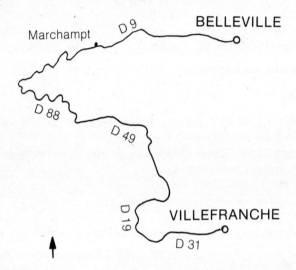

DAY TWO: BELLEVILLE TO FUISSÉ

Today's 40-mile ride takes you up into the Beaujolais hills to some of the famous wine villages, then back into the valley to stay in a wine village whose name is world-famous. The first part of the ride is fairly easy, then the road becomes challenging—with a great culinary and visual reward. We'll start today's ride from the château, so if you've stayed in Taponas, come back into Belleville and follow the directions to the château before continuing.

Go right on D69 from the château entrance. You ride through more rolling vineyards on an easy uphill into **Morgon.**

At the junction with D68, go straight across through Morgon.

(If you are not inclined to take "the high road" today, turn right on D88 in Morgon and rejoin the tour in Villié-Morgon.)

Veer left at the fork.

At the next junction, go left, staying on the main road. The Domaine de la Breche will be on your right as you continue along easy rolling hills.

In Les Chastys, take D78. (sign: Beaujeu) Stay on the main road and on D78 on this uphill grade through the Beaujolais foothills. You'll notice little stone columns topped in yellow by the side of the road. These have the road number painted on them, and can reassure you of the right direction midride.

In Lantignie, where there is a thirteenth-century château, turn left on D78. (sign: Beaujeu) You'll soon come into **Beaujeu,** home of several good wines and the Church of St. Nicholas. You can stop for coffee, or wine tasting, at the Anne de Beaujeu, or visit the caves of Les Vins Gabriel Aligné.

Turn right on D37. (sign: Les Dépôts) This is the main road through Beaujeu, lined with old buildings and flowers.

At the monument, turn right on D136. (sign: Avenas) You'll climb out of town now on moderate to challenging switch-backs all the way to the next junction. Your reward is a magnificent view of the whole valley over your shoulder to the right, then the panorama at the crest of the hill. You'll ride through fragrant forest as the grade lessens. A strategically located hotel which accurately advertises as *"restaurant panoramique"* is a great choice for morning tea or coffee. La Terrasse de Beaujolais (tel. 74-04-20-79) had the *most* incredible selection of fresh fruit tarts, huge berries, meringues, mousse cakes, and other delicacies that we saw anywhere in France.

At the T junction with D18, go right. (sign: Villié-Morgon)

Turn left at the sign to St.-Amour. (Follow the ›› signs to the right.)

Veer right at the fork. Stay on the main road.

In **St.-Amour,** take D186. (signs: Le Bourgneuf, Chénas) In **Le Bourgneuf,** you'll find a multiple juncture.

Take the far left road, which is D31. (sign: Leynes) This section of the ride takes you through beautiful and sweet-smelling woodlands. Stay on D31 into **Leynes.**

There is a climb into the village, where you'll find an interesting wine directory map of the area. We continued on up the slope to stop for lunch at Le Fin Bec (tel. 85-35-60-50). It's unlikely you'll need reservations unless you come in the middle of Sunday lunch rush. If you're in a vegetarian mood, order a plate of delicate fresh vegetables: juicy white asparagus, mushrooms in garlic, au grâtin potatoes, and rice. If not, try a salad of fresh greens and smoked goose breast, followed by a dozen *escargots* redolent of garlic and fresh herbs. The *escargot* was served in a pastry that was light and crisp on top, butter and garlic drenched on the bottom.

Turn right on D172. (sign: Fuissé) You'll ride up over the hill and down into the forest above Fuissé.

At the intersection, go right on D172. (sign: Circuit Pouilly-Fuissé)

A right on D172 will take you into Fuissé. La Vigne Blanche is tonight's hotel. There are many opportunities for wine tasting in this tidy and rich vineyard region.

WHERE TO STAY AND DINE IN FUISSÉ

The two-star La Vigne Blanche is a small, flower-bedecked and proudly run country hotel (71960 Fuissé; tel. 85-35-60-50). You can dine sumptuously there or walk up the road to

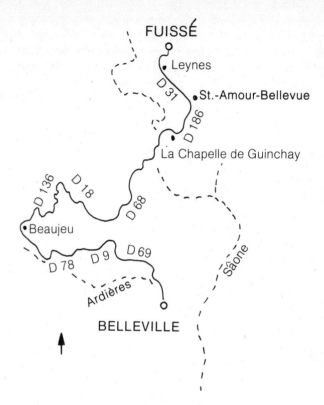

the restaurant Pouilly-Fuissé, which carries a large, regional selection in an airy and comfortable setting. (Modest)

SUMMARY

BURGUNDY-BEAUJOLAIS TOUR: DAY TWO

Belleville to Fuissé

(40 miles)

- Start at the Château de Pizy and go right on D69.
- After about 2 miles, go straight across the junction with D68 in Morgon.

- Veer left at the fork and at the next junction, staying on the main road.
- In less than a mile, take D78 in Les Chastys (sign: Beaujeu).
- After 4 miles into Lantignie, turn left on D78 (sign: Beaujeu).
- Beaujeu comes into view in approximately 2 miles.
- Turn right on D37 (sign: Les Dépôts), then right at the monument on D136 (sign: Avenas) and climb a little over 5 miles.
- At the T junction with D18, go right (sign: Villié-Morgon) for 2 miles, through:
- a left at the sign to St.-Amour;
- a right at the fork, staying on the main road.
- In St.-Amour take D186 (signs: Le Bourgneuf, Chénas) for 2½ miles.
- In Le Bourgneuf, at the multiple juncture, take the far left road, D31 (sign: Leynes).
- Stay on D31 almost 2 miles into Leynes.
- Turn right on D172 (sign: Fuissé).
- At the intersection, go right on D172 (sign: Circuit Pouilly-Fuissé).
- D172 takes you 2 miles into Fuissé.

DAY THREE: FUISSÉ TO BRANCION

This is a spectacular 30-mile day of wine châteaux, sites to visit, and lush back roads in the Mâconnais countryside. The grade is definitely challenging at times as you ride through more outstanding and meticulously tended vineyards and the small villages with the clustered houses that conserve precious land and are characteristic of this area. We'll wind up into the forests of Cluny for lunch and climb into the forests of Brancion at day's end.

Begin today by leaving the hotel and turning left on D172.

Turn right on D209. (sign: Prissé) You'll pass the elegant, old Château de Fuissé on the left.

Go left at fork. (direction: Pouilly)

Take the left following the Solutre signs through Pouilly.

Go straight at the intersection. (sign: Solutre) The charming vistas warrant the steep climb into **Solutre,** where you'll see products of the region when you visit the boutique and several other little shops. The Rock of Solutre, an imposing limestone monument, is visible from the village, where considerable geological excavation has been undertaken. You can stop and visit another French museum, this one of prehistory facts and artifacts. The road continues to climb moderately outside of Solutre. Stay on the main road.

Turn right on D31. (sign: La Grange du Boiss) This road turns into D23 then back into D31, and it heads downhill, sometimes steeply. You'll pass a group of ancient stone buildings into blackberry heaven; this road is lined with vines.

Turn right on D185. (sign: Serrières) A castle is visible in the distance to your right.

Go right at the Château XIVᵉ Siècle sign.

In Pierreclos, go left on D45. (sign: Tramayes)

Take an immediate right on D212. (sign: Milly-Lamartine) You'll have a moderate climb here into **Milly-Lamartine.**
    After a steep downhill takes you a little out of town, you'll see a sign to Cluny.

Take the left fork here. The road winds up and under the busy N79.

Turn right on D17. (sign: Cluny) The uphill grade leads you to a little road that forks to the right. The sign says Berze-le-Châtel. You'll see a château on the hill to your right.

Take the right onto D309 (the back road into Cluny). This small country road climbs steeply for about a mile. In **Berze-le-Châtel,** another medieval château resides in the midst of fields and forest. The road turns into an exhilarating downhill as you enter **Cluny,** home of the famous abbey, and our lunch stop. Cluny is synonymous with the Church splendor of the Middle Ages. First founded in the tenth century by the Duke of Aquitaine, the abbey enjoyed enormous prestige throughout Europe at the height of its influence. At one time it was the largest center of worship in the Christian world. The huge abbey was also accompanied by the biggest church in the world until St. Peter's in Rome eclipsed it by a few yards. Sacked several times, a large part of the abbey was systematically destroyed over the eighteenth and nineteenth centuries. You can still glimpse Cluny's grandeur in the ruins that remain, but they cannot do justice to the power that this center of spiritual activity wielded over the past thousand years. There was a time when the stamp of approval from the Cluny Abbey was enough to ensure political victories and start wars. The view of the town from the Cheese Tower is especially pleasant.

Cluny has many restaurants, and has thoughtfully provided a map of them called "Plan de Cluny," easily available as you enter the abbey environs. We enjoyed the service and food at De Bourgogne (place de l'Abbaye; tel. 85-59-00-58), which is adjacent to the abbey. (Medium)

After lunch, turn right back down the road in front of the abbey.

Turn right on D980. (sign: Mâcon)

Take a left on D15. (sign: Azé) Stay on the D15, which is the route de Vin. The road climbs into the deep, gorgeous forest of the Bois de Bourcier for over a mile. As you top the hill and head down toward Azé you'll see fields outlined with decorative patterns of trees and hedges. A small grotto is available for visiting on your left.

In Azé, turn left on D82. (sign: Lugny)

Take another left on D82. You're now rolling along through level country or gentle hills. You pass through **Bassy,** where you stay on D82 through treasured vineyards. In **St.-Gengoux,** the Caveau de Vieux Logis is open for wine tasting if you'd like a postlunch *digestif.* Small villages abound in this area, and you'll pass through **de Saisse** and **Bonson** before taking another road in **Bissy.**

Turn left on D162. (sign: Cruzielle) You'll cruise through slight up and down elevations as you take the middle road through the wine and château country. In **Cruzielle,** you'll pass an elegant château on your left. The vineyards here are sprinkled among the fields.

In **Martailly-lès-Brancion** turn left at the first fork onto D14. (sign: Chapaize) This is your final climb of the day through the Mâconnais region. The last cozy village is visible over your shoulder as you pedal up into **Brancion.**

WHERE TO STAY AND DINE IN BRANCION

We have three selections for you in different price ranges and with varying ambiance:

To sample the medieval village directly, make reservations for one of the ten rooms of the Auberge du Vieux Brancion (François de Murard, Brancion, 71700 Tournus; tel. 85-51-03-83). You will travel back in time in the beamed ceiling rooms with stone floors in this authentic fifteenth-century house. A popular stop for meals, we found the dining room full of cyclists enjoying rich Burgundian fare. The old walled feudal market town has been well restored and preserved, and the site itself, high on a rock ridge overlooking the area, is worth the visit. The old castle, church, and restored houses are open to the public daily from Easter through mid-November. The rest of the year visits are available only on Sundays and holidays. (Modest)

Across the road and up a short hill you'll find the spacious and elegant La Montagne de Brancion, a three-star hotel (Brancion, 71700 Tournus; tel. 85-51-12-40). The view of the other side of the hill from this hotel is quite beautiful, and their advertised *"grand calme"* is accurate. If you like quiet, restful gardens, a pool to refresh your traveling legs, and a patio where you can eat breakfast, you might enjoy La Montagne. This hotel has no restaurant, but does serve breakfast. (Medium)

The Auberge du Col de Brancion (tel. 85-51-00-84) is right on the main road. You can sample the local color in their hospitable dining area, where many travelers stop. The rooms come with showers.

Up the road about three miles on the D14 in Chapaize is another famous eleventh-century Romanesque church that you may want to visit in the morning before continuing. Glorified by the prestige of Cluny, the simplicity of this church affords an interesting comparison to the elaborations of latter century churches.

SUMMARY

BURGUNDY-BEAUJOLAIS TOUR: DAY THREE

Fuissé to Brancion

(30 miles)

- Begin in front of the hotel La Vigne Blanche and turn left on D172.
- Turn right on D209 (sign: Prissé).
- Go left at the fork.
- Take the left following the Solutre signs through Pouilly, going straight at the intersection 2 miles into Solutre.
- Turn right on D31 (sign: La Grange du Boiss), which turns into D23 and back into D31 for a little over 3 miles.
- Turn right on D185 (sign: Serrières) and ride over 2 miles into Pierreclos.
- Go left on D45 (sign: Tramayes).
- Take an immediate right on D212 (sign: Milly-Lamartine) and continue for 2½ miles into Milly-Lamartine.

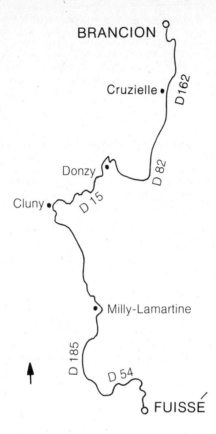

- Take the left fork at the sign to Cluny.
- Turn right on D17 for about 3 miles.
- Take the right onto D309 (the back road into Cluny).
- After a steep 1-mile climb into Berzé-le-Châtel, the road winds downhill about 3½ miles into Cluny for lunch and sightseeing.
- After lunch, turn back down the road in front of the abbey.
- Turn right on D980 (sign: Mâcon).
- After a short distance, turn left on D15 (sign: Azé) and follow the route de Vin for over 7 miles into Azé.
- In Azé turn left on D82 (sign: Lugny), and take another left to stay on D82.
- 3½ miles takes you through Bassy and into St.-Gengoux on D82.

- Stay on D82 another 2 miles into Bissy, where you'll turn left on D162 (sign: Cruzille).
- In 3½ miles you'll pass Cruzille and come into Martailly-les-Brancion.
- Take a left at the first fork onto D14 (sign: Chapaize). The final climb of the day is less than 1 mile.

DAY FOUR: BRANCION TO CHAGNY

After yesterday's climbs you'll be amazed at how flat the territory is today. We promise only two serious hills in this otherwise flat, 40-mile day of river valley and small villages, culminating at one of the best hotel-restaurants in France.

Begin today's ride by turning onto D14. (direction: Chapaize)

Turn left on D149 at the Auberge du Col de Brancion. (direction: La Chapelle) Stay on the main road in this downhill section. The purpose of this morning's ride is to transport you into more wine country. The smooth, fairly level road carries you through many pastoral scenes of little villages set among farmland.

In **Collonge, turn left on D215.** (sign: St.-Gengoux)

In **Nogent, turn right on D159.** (sign: Sennecey) Stay on the main road here through several small back roads. Wind through the town of **Tallant.**

Turn onto D67.
     Stay on D67 through **Sully.**

In **Nanton, turn left on D147.** (sign: La Chapelle-de-Bragny) The road leads into some lightly forested areas on your way into la Chapelle.

Take a left on D6. (sign: Bresse)

Go right on D147. (sign: Messey-sur-Grosne) You'll pass over a beautiful little stream here, typical of this area of France, where surprising scenes and memorable images greet you at each turn. In **Messey-le-Bois,** we saw a group of men enjoying what looked like a long-standing game of *boule.*

Turn onto D49 here. (signs: Chalon, Buxy) Stay on D49 through the forest of la Ferté. A pretty little valley leads into **St.-Germain-les-Buxy.**

Turn left on D104 at the monument.

At the junction with D977, cross, staying on D104. (sign: Givry) The road travels up over the N80.

Turn right onto D981. (sign: Givry)

As you come into the pleasant town of Givry, follow the Toutes Directions signs, then the signs toward Chagny, to take you into town for lunch. The Hôtel du Midi is in the center of town. We counted at least two *boulangeries* for lighter fare. You may enjoy some of the popular Givry wine with lunch, a favorite *vin ordinaire* of Henri IV. If you walk around a little, you may see some of the town's many fountains, the masterful Gauthey church, or the prosperous-looking town hall.

Go back out of town, taking a right on D170. (sign: Jambles) You'll thread your way through old villages and vineyards, remaining on D170.

Stay right on D170. (sign: Moroges) You are now entering some more serious wine-tasting country, where for the rest of the afternoon you'll be tempted by various châteaux and cellars.

Turn right at the Barizy, St.-Denis sign. You'll go uphill for a short stretch here through the village of **Jambles.**

Follow the signs to St. Denis-de-Vaux on a white gravel road through the forest.

In **St.-Denis** turn right at the iron gates of the château. Vineyards grace the hills to your right.

Veer right at the fork onto D48. (sign: Mellecey)

Just before the charming village of Mellecey, turn left at the sign to St.-Martin-sous-Montaigu. You have a short, steep climb here with an old stone wall to your left.

At the stop sign, go left. You'll shortly see the sign for D155, which lets you know you're on the right road into **St.-Martin.**

In this vineyard country, go right at the next intersection. (sign: Itineraire Recommendre) Ride straight through town. An occasional sign will say D155.

Turn left at **Touches.** Stay on the main road, which will rise through the vineyards. There are great views of small villages to your left through this section of your ride.

At the X intersection, go straight past a church on your right and wind around to the right. Don't take the steep downhill to the left.

Turn left at the stone cross obelisk.

Go left at the Bourchard Ainé et fils sign on the wall. You'll find that this series of back roads has taken you into the famous wine village of **Mercurey,** where there is a profusion of opportunities for wine tasting. The road bends downhill for a bit.

Take the right fork onto D978. (sign: Charrecey) You have another slight uphill climb after your downhill rest.

Go right at the fork onto D109. (sign: Aluze) The road becomes hill and dale for a stretch here as you come into the village of **Aluze,** which overlooks the valley. Stay on D109 as you head downhill again through hedge-defined fields. The Domaine du Chantilly château is visible to your left. On the day we last took the D109, we didn't encounter a single car.

In **Remigny,** go right on D974 all the way into **Chagny.**

WHERE TO STAY AND DINE IN CHAGNY

We've ended the day here to give you the opportunity to experience one of the best restaurants in Burgundy and probably in all of France. The Hôtel Lameloise, an old mansion in the heart of Chagny, has exquisitely appointed rooms, a hushed and reverent ambiance, and a dedicated staff (36 place d'Armes, 71150 Chagny-en-Bourgogne; tel. 85-87-08-85). Reserve both your room and meals well ahead. This stay will be an event, and is well worth its price. The last time we were there, the set 295 francs (about $50) lunch menu included a salad of artichokes and *foie gras, escargot*, roast lamb with saffron, duck breast in black currant sauce, plus the usual amenities. The à la carte menu offered steamed turbot in truffle butter sauce and warm lemon soufflé for two. The set dinner menu is in the $70–90 per person range. A mouth-watering finale to your day. (Medium–Top)

Another tempting choice, for its graceful pastoral setting, is the Auberge du Camp Romain (Chassey-le-Camp, 71150 Chagny; tel. 85-87-09-91). This hotel offers twenty-five rooms, very respectable Burgundian fare, and the pleasures of the countryside. Turn onto the D109 from the D974 to reach this little gem. (Modest–Low Medium)

SUMMARY

BURGUNDY-BEAUJOLAIS TOUR: DAY FOUR

Brancion to Chagny

(40 miles)

- Strike out on D14 toward Chapaize.
- Shortly, turn left on D149 at the Auberge du Col de Brancion (direction: La Chapelle).
- After about 2 miles, in Collonge, turn left on D215 (sign: St.-Gengoux) and ride about 1 mile.
- In Nogent turn right on D159 (sign: Sennecey) 3 miles to Tallant.
- Turn onto D67 and ride through Sully 1½ miles to Nanton.
- Turn left on D147 (sign: la Chapelle-de-Bragny) for 2½ miles.
- Turn left on D6 (sign: Bresse) and shortly, right on D147 (sign: Messey-sur-Grosne) and cycle for 1½ miles into Messey-le-Bois.
- Turn on D49 (signs: Chalon, Buxy) about 4½ miles into St.-Germain-les-Buxy.
- Turn left on D104 at the monument, and follow D104 about 7 miles to the next junction.
- Turn right onto D981 (sign: Givry) into Givry for lunch.
- Turn right on D170 (sign: Jambles) for about 2½ miles, turning right at the Barizy, St.-Denis sign and going into Jambles.
- Follow the signs to St.-Denis-de-Vaux on a white gravel road for about 2 miles.
- In St.-Denis, turn right at the gates of the château and veer right at the fork onto D48 (sign: Mellecey) for about 2 miles.
- Turn left at the sign to St.-Martin-sous-Montaigu.
- At the stop sign, go left onto D155 a short distance into St.-Martin.
- Stay on D155 (occasionally marked) into Touches.
- Turn left at Touches, staying on the main road. Go straight past a church on your right at the X intersection, turn left at the stone cross obelisk, and go left at the Bourchard Aine et Fils sign, which all take you the back 2 miles into Mercurey.
- Take the right fork onto D978 (sign: Charrecey) for less than a mile.
- Go right at the fork onto D109 (sign: Aluze) for 6 miles.
- In Remigny, go right on D974 for less than 2 miles into Chagny.

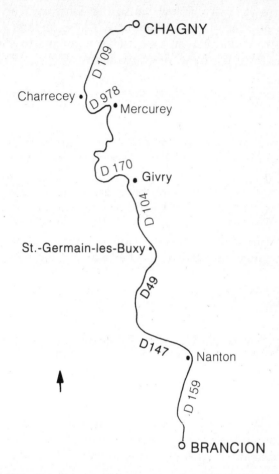

DAY FIVE: CHAGNY TO BEAUNE

In this wine-wandering day you'll get an intimate look at some of the most famous wine villages in France (and therefore the world) as we head into the Côte de Beaune. The roads in this 38-mile ride are level to moderate, with a few short challenging hills to take you to the best views of vineyards and valleys.

Begin today on the D974. (direction: Remigny)

At the stop sign, follow the sign to Santenay. The D113 takes you into the village of **Santenay,** whose underground mineral waters contribute an essential component to the reputable wine from the large vineyards here.

Follow the D113 through town, turning at the Santenay-le-Haut sign.

Take a right fork on the D113. (sign: Decize) You come into some uphill territory here through the vineyards.

Turn right at the fork onto D136. (sign: Decize) Breeze through the village of **Decize** on one especially steep downhill.

Go right at the fork. (sign: Nolay) You're still on D136, which you follow into **Nolay** and the official Côte de Beaune.

In **Paris l'Hôpital,** go left on D136. (signs: Sivry, Route des Vins)

Turn left on D225. (signs: St.-Sernin, Route des Vins) Stay on D225, where the fairly steep uphill is rewarded with a great view of the valley.

In **St.-Sernin-du-Plain,** turn right on D225. (sign: Mazenay)

Make two rights at the next two forks. (sign: Mazenay) A brief excursion into rich agricultural land leads you into **Mazenay.**

Go right onto D1. (sign: Nolay) The road gently rises and falls as it leads you into the tree-lined streets of **Nolay.**
    This sunny and bright town is your lunch stop. There are several very clean restaurants and *boulangeries* from which to choose. The Gril restaurant's menu is in English, offering Burgundy meat specialties such as beef in red wine, sausage, the ubiquitous *escargot* (in a pie here), and luscious desserts. Walking sights include the ancient covered market and a fifteenth-century church.

Following lunch, turn right on the D973. (sign: La Rochepot) The blissfully smooth road takes you on an uphill grade over the junction with N73 and through verdant hills. The Relais du Château is on your right as you come into the *centre ville* of **La Rochepot.**

We recommend ascending the town to the twelfth-century château perched atop it. The last section of road to the castle is quite steep, and all the panting cyclists in our tour a few years ago were quite disgruntled to find the castle closed on the Tuesday we rode there. If you arrive on another day, you'll find this restored château accessible by a weathered drawbridge, with many treasures illuminating its interior. We enjoyed the ride through the village and trees to the château as much as the tour itself.

(*Note:* We want to make special mention here that the next section of road is tricky to negotiate because some of the signs are inconspicuous. Be patient.)

Leave La Rochepot on D973. (direction: Nolay)

Turn left on D33 at the X junction. (sign: St.-Aubin) You'll see a magnificent view of La Rochepot to your left as you climb out of town on the high road of Burgundy. The glittering rooftops of the villages lead you downhill into **St.-Aubin.** (Don't go on the N6 here.)

Go left into town, staying toward the right at the fork.

At the stone monument, take the left fork, continuing into the valley.

At the next fork, veer right.

In the little village of Gamay, go left at the T intersection on the bridge. You'll be riding uphill on an unmarked street here.

Turn right at the sign to Blagny. You'll see Gamay over your right shoulder as you climb steeply through vineyards on this little country road.

Turn right at the T fork, following the road around to the left through this little village. The road becomes wider and paved here.

At the X intersection of the walled château, go left.

At the next T intersection, go right past a forest on your right and vineyards on your left.

At the next T junction, head left between waist-high walls of the vineyards. You'll see a village ahead and toward the right. You are riding through the vineyards that supply the famous white and subtle red Montrachet wine. The road passes through villages with one renowned name after another here, with many opportunities to stop and sample.

You may notice as you head into Burgundy territory that the vine tending becomes manicured. The more celebrated the grapes, the more impeccably they are tended. You may want to take the time to study the wine classification and labeling process. In general, there are three different classifications. The *Village* wines, the least controlled and more *ordinaire*, are labeled by village name only. *Première Cru* wines are labeled with both the name of the village and the vineyard name. *Grand Cru* wines need only the vineyard name, and earn their fame with the tenderest coddling. We enjoyed all the wines we sampled, and encourage you to follow your nose in exploring this ancient wine culture.

Turn left on D113 B. (sign: Meursault) Wind through the prosperous town of **Meursault** and, if you wish, taste wines at one of several cellars. One possible hotel for tonight is located in Meursault. (We describe it below.)

Turn left at the sign to Ligny.

Take a right on D23. (sign: Monthelie)

Turn right on D11B. (sign: Beaune) You'll join the larger road here with signs to Beaune and Pommard. Note the large Volnay sign to your right, indicating the vineyards that produce this popular wine. You'll ride through **La Chapelle** and **Pommard,** where there is a large château on your right.

Turn left onto the busy N74. (sign: Beaune) You'll be on this heavily trafficked but direct route into Beaune for a little over a mile. (*Note:* There is a bike path down the left side on N74. We recommend using it.)

Take your first Centre Ville sign into Beaune.

WHERE TO STAY AND DINE IN BEAUNE

We have spent hours walking through Beaune and sampling the wares of various shops and restaurants. Beaune is another French city whose walled heart is circumscribed by busy peripheral streets. Once you are inside the perimeter, Beaune has a cosmopolitan and stately air, with cobbled streets and a pedestrian mall.

There are many things to see and do in this wine capital. The Hôtel Dieu, which is an ornate former charity hospital built after the incredible devastation of the Hundred Years' War, is near the tourist information center. You can see examples of how far medicine has come in five hundred years, as well as the almost Eastern-looking roof, the elaborate interior decor, and several famous works of art. Another French museum, this one of the whole history of Burgundy wine, is housed in the former home of the dukes of Burgundy. Beaune has its own Notre Dame church, an offshoot of Cluny begun in the twelfth century. The well-proportioned and lovely architecture contains large doors reminiscent of Cluny, beautiful stained-glass, and the intricate *Tapestries of the Life of the Virgin Mary*. Also, in wandering around town, you'll find grand old houses, parks and waterways, genial shopkeepers, and many opportunities to observe the daily rhythms of this wine center.

One pleasant hotel in central Beaune is Le Cep, which you'll pass just after coming into the central area of Beaune.

(27 rue Maufoux; tel. 80-22-35-48). Built around a courtyard, many of its sumptuous rooms have balconies for eating breakfast. It has all of the things we most appreciate when traveling: large firm beds, good reading light, lavish bathroom fixtures, warmth, and a friendly staff. You'll find generous accommodations, delectable Burgundian cuisine, and easy access to central Beaune. (Medium)

For those desiring country lodging in style, Le Chevreuil et la mère Daugier is an impeccably maintained nineteenth-century château with twenty rooms in Meursault (Face à l'Hôtel del Ville, 21190 Meursault; tel. 80-21-23-25). A two-star establishment run by the entire Thevenot family, Le Chevreuil's renowned menu can be sampled on its terrace or in the pleasant dining room. (Medium)

There are many fine restaurants in and around Beaune in whatever price range you desire. You may wish to consult the many guides available at the tourist information center, or wander and see where your eyes and nose lead you. Some restaurants we can recommend are the two-star Relais de la Diligence (21190 Meursault Gare; tel. 80-21-21-32), Relais de la Madeleine (44 place Madeleine; tel. 80-22-07-47), and the beautifully decorated Relais de Saulx, 6 rue Louis-Very; tel. 80-22-01-35).

SUMMARY

BURGUNDY-BEAUJOLAIS TOUR: DAY FIVE

Chagny to Beaune

(35–40 miles)

- Begin on the D974 toward Remigny.
- At the stop sign, follow the sign 2 miles to Santenay on D113.
- Follow the D113 through town and take a right fork on D113 (sign: Decize) and again at D136 for 2½ miles into Decize.

- Go right at the fork (sign: Nolay) on D136 for 2 miles.
- In Paris l'Hôpital, go left on D136 (signs: Sivry, Route des Vins).
- Turn left on D225 shortly (signs: St.-Sernin, Route des Vins).
- Stay on D225 through St.-Sernin du Plain and Mazenay for about 3 miles.
- Go right on D1 (sign: Nolay) for 3½ miles into Nolay and lunch.
- Turn right on the D973 (sign: La Rochepot) the 2½ miles into La Rochepot.
- Leave La Rochepot on D973 (direction: Nolay).
- In town still, turn left on D33 at the X juncture (sign: St.-Aubin) and ride for 3 miles into St.-Aubin.
- Go left into town and stay right at the fork.
- At the stone monument, take the left fork, continuing into the valley.
- At the next fork, veer right and into the village of Gamay.
- Go left at the T intersection on the bridge.
- Turn right at the sign to Blagny and right at the T fork.
- The couple of miles of back roads into Montrachet are as follows: go left at the X intersection of the walled château; right at the next T intersection with forest on your right and vineyards on your left, left at the next T between waist-high walls of vineyards.

- Turn left on D113B (sign: Meursault) for less than a mile into Meursault.
- Turn left at the sign to Ligny and right on D23 (sign: Monthelie).
- Take the right on D11B (sign: Beaune) 3 miles, through La Chapelle and Pommard.
- Turn left on the N74 for a little over a mile into Beaune.

DAY SIX: BEAUNE TO GEVREY-CHAMBERTIN

Today's 30–35-mile ride combines hillside climbs with vineyard viewing. You'll begin with a challenging forested section, then move into rolling vineyard country. The cuisine available today sets an even higher standard for beauty, elegance, and taste. The variety of countryside and the prominence of the grapes you'll pass may make your head spin, even if you don't sample.

This is the heart of Burgundy. Savor it.

Leave Beaune going north on N74. Look for the D18 sign, which will be on your left on the side of the corner store, La Chaussonerie.

Turn left on D18.

At the fork, go right. (sign: Bouilland)

Turn left onto D2. (sign: Bouilland) After **Savigny-lès-Beaune,** a pretty, flowered and garden-bedecked village, the road begins a long, moderately graded ten-mile climb through deep, rich forest and fields all the way into Bouilland. The D2 follows the Rhoin River, which nourishes the tall trees and deep grasses of this area. We have scheduled your lunch stop here in Bouilland both because the restaurant is so good and because you have a steep climb after lunch. If your appetite is not quite ripe when you arrive in Bouilland, go and visit the ruins of the sixteenth-century Abbey of St. Marguerite, which is just below the tiny village. The Hostellerie du Vieux Moulin, run by Isabelle and Jean-Pierre Silva, is open for lunch from 12–2 P.M. (tel. 80-21-51-16). You enter the restaurant on a bridge over a fish-filled stream, and the windows of the large dining room overlook the gardens. We have had delicious meals here, including the best fish dish in our experience: braised trout in a delicate sauce capped with roasted slivers of leek. Feel free to indulge; you'll need the fuel for the next climb.

Turn left at the sign to Pouilly. You'll see immediately why we recommended eating heartily. Pace yourself and remember your breathing.

Stay right as you come out of town.

Turn right at the Poterie sign. You're back into field and forest country again, climbing steeply for a few miles.

Go right on D18. (sign: Beaune) The road levels out here through this peaceful and untraveled region.

Go left on D25. (sign: Bruant)

In Bruant, turn right staying on D25. This is the Haut Côtes de Nuits, the high country of Burgundy. You'll ride through the village of **Ascenant.**

Here, follow the D25 signs. (signs: Meuilley, Nuits-St.-Georges)

Turn right on D115. (sign: Villers-la-Faye) The alternating fields and woods here are moderately hilly.

In Marrey-lès-Fussey, turn left on D8. (sign: Nuits-St.-Georges) The forest becomes even more lush here, the hills rolling and endless. Ride through the town of **Chaux.**

Go right at the fork on D8. (sign: Nuits-St.-Georges) The road rolls gently downhill here, overlooking the famous vineyards and pleasing town of Nuits-St.-Georges, where world-renowned wine has been produced for a thousand years. There are many wine-sampling treats available here if you want to ride into town. We will take you around the edge of town to avoid N74.

Angle left at the signs for Meuilley and Villar.

Take a left onto D25.

At the stop sign go left. You'll pass through a lovely residential area.

Head right at the fork onto D109. (sign: Concoeur) The road stretches into a long hill here into **Concoeur,** where it winds up through the village, down through forest, and opens into vineyards. You'll enter next the familiarly named village of **Vosnée-Romanée,** home of world-famous delightfully light red wines. You may be amazed, as we were, to see how much great wine is produced on so little acreage.

Turn left at the sign: 5 Ver N74. Go across N74 and under the railroad crossing.

Take the first left through the vineyards. This small road takes you into **Flagey-Echezeaux.**

Turn left onto D109. (sign: Gilly)

In Gilly, head left at the Château du Gilly sign.

Take another left at the sign to Vougeot.

Turn right onto D25h. (sign: Vougeot)

Take an immediate left on D25. (sign: Vougeot) The road takes you over the railroad tracks and the N74, then into **Vougeot.**

At the stop sign turn right.

Turn left on D122. (sign: Route des Grand Crus) The Route of the Great Wines will take you all the way into Gevrey-Chambertin. While still in Vougeot, you may want to stop and see one of the most well-known château of the area, the twelfth-century Clos de Vougeot château. The property of the Citeaux abbey for several centuries, in this century the château has become the home of the Brotherhood of the Knights of the Tastevin. Several hundred people meet regularly in the Great Cellar with great ritual to promote the regional wines, and the well-attended wine festivals are coordinated with the celebrations in Beaune.

Follow the D122 signs (don't take the D122H route) into Morey-St.-Denis. There are yet more wine-tasting options here, and all along this famous road.

Continue following the Route des Grand Cru signs into Gevrey-Chambertin, whose wine was Napoleon's favorite.

WHERE TO STAY AND DINE IN THE GRAND CRU REGION

One place we've selected for you to stay is a perfect jewel of the Grand Cru villages, aptly named Les Grands Crus (Route des Grand Crus, 21220 Gevrey-Chambertin; tel. 80-34-34-15). Signs easily lead you to this modern, country hotel which overlooks the vineyards and the old château. Its flowering vine-covered walls house comfortable rooms, a large, beamed sitting room with carved fireplace and tile floors, and some of the best croissants in France. You can breakfast in the garden. Within walking distance of the best restaurants in the region, this hotel has twenty-four rooms, all with baths and phones. (Moderate)

If your tastes run more toward renovated châteaux, the Castel Tres Girard located on the A31 just past St.-Denis may be perfect for you (Morey-St.-Denis, 21220 Gevrey-Chambertin; tel. 80-34-33-09). The vine-covered walls of this eighteenth-century château house rustic yet elegant rooms, some decorated in Louis XIII style, a large dining room serving course after course of delectable Burgundian cuisine, and vineyard views. (Moderate)

We usually eat at Les Millesimes when we're in the area, but on our last trip we decided to try something different. Close to the center of town, La Sommellerie is beautifully and simply decorated and focuses on food, not pomp and circumstance (7 rue Souvert, 21220 Gevrey-Chambertin; tel. 80-34-31-48). We began with a simple salad of four different greens, fresh green beans, and herbs in a finely spiced vinaigrette, and *rissoles de foie gras*. These gorgeous little puff pastries were filled with *foie gras* and truffles, and floated in a burgundy sauce. We continued with meltingly tender scallops of lamb with whole garlic (a harmonious marriage of tastes) and ravioli stuffed with lobster, served in a sauce of the lobster's own juices. Desserts were cold nougat ice cream with puréed pear sauce and chocolate mousse. It was close to the top of our all-time great dinners in France. (Modest–Moderate)

If you're interested in an *haute cuisine* experience, you cannot top Les Millesimes (25 rue de l'Eglise and rue de Meixville; tel. 80-51-84-24), a converted wine warehouse right around the corner from the Hôtel les Grand Crus. One meal here occupied four hours, with the complete replacement of silver and place setting between each exquisite course. You enter the seventeenth-century Les Millesimes through the arched iron doorway, and if you're lucky enough to obtain reservations, dine in the converted wine cellar. You can easily dine into the Top range, which ensures the appearance of several wines with dinner and fresh dessert pastries, dessert proper, *and* chocolate truffles with coffee. We recommend everything, especially braised duck, brochette of salmon and *foie gras*, fresh fish with unique sauces, or whatever the genial hosts suggest. The cheese table is a meal in itself, from which you will experience provocative tastes that are unavailable in the United States due to our pasteurizing laws. We have not seen an abundance of vegetables at the *haute cuisine* tables in

France, and salad seems relegated to two-star status, so be prepared to surrender to indulgence and get your fiber elsewhere. (Top)

SUMMARY

BURGUNDY-BEAUJOLAIS TOUR: DAY SIX

Beaune to Gevrey-Chambertin

(30–35 miles)

- Exit Beaune on N74 north.
- Look for and turn left at the D18 sign at the corner store, La Chaussonerie.
- At the fork after a few hundred feet, go right (sign: Bouilland).
- Turn onto D2 after 2½ miles (sign: Bouilland).
- After a mile into Savigny-lès-Beaune, stay on D2 for 10 miles into Bouilland for lunch.
- Turn left at the sign to Pouilly.
- Stay right as you come out of town.
- Turn right at the Poterie sign and climb for a few miles.
- Take a right on D18 (sign: Beaune).
- Go left on D25 (sign: Bruant) after less than a mile.
- In Bruant, turn right, staying on D25 for about 3 miles through Ascenant, and following the signs to Meuilley and Nuits-St.-Georges.
- Turn right on D115 (sign: Villers-la-Faye) for 1½ miles.
- In Marrey-lès-Fussey, turn left and stay on D8 (sign: Nuits-St.-Georges) for about 4 miles through Chaux and above Nuits.
- Angle left at the signs for Meuilley and Villar.
- Take a left onto D25.
- At the stop sign go left for a few blocks.
- Head right at the fork onto D109 (sign: Concoeur) for almost 2 miles into Concoeur and, just after, Vosnée-Romanée.
- Turn left at the sign: 5 Ver N74, crossing N74 and under the railroad crossing.
- Take the first left through the vineyards less than a mile into Flagey-Echezeaux.

- Turn left onto D109 (sign: Gilly).
- After less than one mile, head left at the Château du Gilly sign.
- Take another left at the sign to Vougeot.
- Turn right onto D25h and an immediate left on D25 (sign: Vougeot).
- In Vougeot, turn right on D122 at the stop sign (route des Grand Crus). This route takes you the remaining 3 miles into Gevrey-Chambertin.

GEVREY-CHAMBERTIN

Morey-St.-Denis

Meuilley

D 25

Bouilland

D 109

Vosnée Romanée

Nuits-St.-Georges

D 8

D 2

Savigny-lès-Beaune

D 18

BEAUNE

D 122

DAY SEVEN: GEVREY-CHAMBERTIN TO DIJON

The short ride into Dijon on the D122 should give you time to hop the TGV to Paris in the afternoon (be sure to make advance reservations). If you decide to stay another day to explore Dijon, home of the former dukes of Burgundy, or to take side trips, we recommend a hotel.

The direction today is simple: stay on D122 all the way into Dijon. You'll pass through **Brochon,** home of more excellent wines. Next comes **Fixin,** whose wines compete favorably with the best of Côte de Nuits. You'll find another museum here containing memorabilia of Napoleon's campaigns and stairs up to a good view of the Saône Valley and the surrounding mountains. You'll ride into **Marsannay-la-Côte,** another famous village which produces rosé wine from Pinot Noir grapes. Shortly comes **Chenôve,** late home of the vast wine cellars of the dukes of Burgundy. And then you'll notice more congestion and signs that indicate the imminent appearance of **Dijon.**

WHERE TO STAY AND DINE IN DIJON

A restful hotel in central Dijon is the Hostellerie du Chapeau Rouge (5 rue Michelet, 21000 Dijon; tel. 80-30-28-10). Its thirty-three rooms are filled with antiques as well as modern conveniences, and its atrium has a tropical feeling with its many plants and sun-filled windows. The restaurant is well-regarded, and you'll find easy access to Dijon's sights from its doors. Many other hotels are listed at the tourist information center.

SUMMARY

BURGUNDY-BEAUJOLAIS TOUR: DAY SEVEN

Gevrey-Chambertin to Dijon

(7–10 miles—depending on sidetrips)

- The basic direction: stay on D122 all the way into Dijon.
- You'll pass Brochon, Fixin, Marsannay-la-Côte, and Chenôve as you ride the vineyards into Dijon.

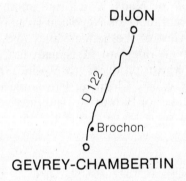

ALSACE:

MOUNTAINS

AND FLOWERS

EMPHATICALLY FRENCH BUT WITH A STRONG GERMAN influence, this region has a flavor all its own. For most of its long history, Alsace has been ruled by Germany (and you could go to jail here even a hundred years ago for using a French word). Since 1945, of course, the region has been French, but before that there was always a tug-of-war over who would have influence over this beautiful area. There is quite a bit of rivalry here still between the Alsatians and the Germans right across the border, in spite of the fact that Alsace eats German food and speaks a German dialect. This was the only area in France where our conversation attempts were regularly misunderstood, necessitating more mime and pointing. It is a wonderful place to ride. We like to visit here in the spring or fall, when the colors are at their best, and the crowds are not as much in evidence. Our tour takes us along the main wine route, with the prettiest vineyards in all of France, and, in stunning contrast, up into the majestic forested mountains of the highlands. Flowers and berry bushes line the roads, as do ancient towers and ramparts of the region's medieval past. The wine villages have a distinctive gingerbread architecture reminiscent of Switzerland, and the architecture of the highland towns is heavier and more somber than the light, French feeling of most French villages. In the summer season many of the villages illuminate themselves by night, making for great late evening rides.

THE FOOD AND WINE OF ALSACE

The food here is unlike anywhere else in France. The flavor is Germanic, with lots of sausages and dumplings in evidence. We did find, however, that *escargots* and fine sauces are as pervasive here as elsewhere in France. The Alsatians make creative use of all sorts of odd portions of animal anatomy; as the saying goes, nothing is left of the pig "but his squeal." You won't have to look hard to find the *andouille* sausage, recently brought to Americans' attention through the popularity of Cajun cooking. The spicy *andouille*, resting on a bed of sauerkraut, makes a hearty dinner on a chilly fall night. We had never liked sauerkraut (here called *choucroute*, its French name) before coming to Alsace. Here they raise this simple dish to a fine art. The Alsatians also love fresh white cheeses. The Alsatian bakery is a bounteous joy to behold, too. They love fruit tarts of various kinds; be on the lookout also for a moist cinnamony roll called *kranz*.

The wines of the region are world famous. The hallmark tastes are light, fruity, and fragrant. We like a glass of crisp, sweetish Riesling in the evening when we're in Alsace. The beer here is uniformly excellent, thanks to German brewing expertise. If you like stronger spirits, the Alsatians also make a variety of liqueurs out of the local mountain berries.

DAY ONE: COLMAR TO MUNSTER

The Alsace tour begins in the sophisticated city of Colmar, which boasts both medieval and Renaissance architecture,

parks, and gardens. The trip from Paris, leaving from the
Gare de l'Est, takes five hours or so. Colmar has a definite
German style, from heavier architecture to heavier food, and
is a curious mixture of charming and dull. It is another walled
city, with cobblestone streets running through much of the
old section. The center of the city is filled with shops and
boutiques of a more international flavor than elsewhere in
France. Its Musée d'Unterlinden is well visited and quite famous. Several churches and beautiful old homes are worth
seeing, as is the museum-home of Bartholdi, creator of the
Statue of Liberty. Be advised that *everything* commercial
rather than culinary, even the office of tourist information, 4
rue des Unterlinden (tel. 89-41-02-29), closes between noon
and 2.

If your train ride from Paris brings you into Colmar late
in the day, we can recommend the Hotel Bristol, a three-star
delight right across from the large train station (place de la
Gare, 68025 Colmar; tel. 89-23-59-59). It has seventy rooms,
furnished in a combination of eighteenth-century period style,
and modern French touches such as color TV, refrigerated
bar, and direct-dial phones. The dining room is beamed and
quite elegant, serving a wide variety of Alsatian specialties.
(Moderate–Top)

The Hostellerie Le Marechal is located near the Lauch
River (4–5 place des Six-Montagnes-Noires, 68000 Colmar;
tel. 89-41-60-32), and is the interesting maze-like result of
joining three sixteenth-century homes. You'll find the rooms
here simpler and more rustic. The restaurant serves veal and
game bird dishes as well as more traditional Alsatian dishes.
(Moderate–Low Top)

DAY ONE: COLMAR TO MUNSTER

You'll start this 35-mile day by touring the wine country. The
wine villages of Alsace are fairly closely spaced, giving you
many opportunities to view and taste. Some of the wine-tasting places offer Eau de Vie, a stronger, fruit-flavored brandy.
In the afternoon you'll earn your cheese as you climb steadily

through the mountains' thick, verdant forests. The forests in Alsace are like overstuffed furniture, spilling over in their round abundance, whereas the forests in Provence are more craggy and tenacious. The last time we took this mountain road we passed only a handful of cars the whole length of it.

Take a right on the road in front of the train station (south).

Turn right on Quartier Sud. Stay on this street; you will be on D30. Ride up over the rue Nationale and on for about 200 feet.

Go right at the next junction. (sign: Equisheim)

Go across the next juncture, which places you on D14. (sign: Husseren) You'll quickly come into the ancient, archetypically authentic village of **Equisheim.** A wine-tasting feast, Equisheim boasts a couple of picturesque churches, three tall towers called the Châteaux du Haut Equisheim, and, of course, many photo opportunities of the traditional village scene. You'll begin to notice that all the wine villages appear to have hired the same architect, who must have had German, Swiss, Belgian, and French heritage. The stone walls of most of the houses and stores have the traditional uncovered wood beams, painted shutters, ornamental windows, and cutout window boxes filled with bright begonias.

Turn left at the Husseren-les-Châteaux sign. (You'll stay on D14.) The road turns steadily uphill in this section, passing **Husseren-les-Châteaux**, the peak of this end of the wine route and the beginning of panoramic views.

Turn here onto D1. (sign: Route of the five châteaux) At this point you are halfway up the slopes and have a good view of the valley.

At the intersection, stay on D1. (sign: Obermorschwihr) We'll begin heading downhill here for a bit as the road winds into **Obermorschwihr.** You'll next come to **Herrlisheim-près-Col-**

mar, home of the remaining ramparts called the *Schelmen-turn*, or, "good for nothing" tower.

Take the right on D1 XI. (sign: Gueberschwihr) Keep following the signs to **Gueberschwihr**, where you will see many well-maintained wine-growers' homes and may stop to more closely examine the magnificent Romanesque clock.

Follow the signs to Centre Ville.

In the center of town, take the road to the left of the building that says Vins Alsace Clement Werck. Ride past the *forge des arts* on your right.

Follow the Pfaffenheim sign out through vineyards. If you've been elsewhere in France, you'll notice that the thicker vines here are allowed to roam more wildly, giving the vineyards a more abandoned air than the tidy vineyards of Burgundy.

At the stop sign, go left down into the village of Pfaffenheim. Keep to the right as you wend through the village.

Turn for a short distance on the N83. (sign: Rouffach) We apologize for this stretch of trafficky road. The alternative is very steep, so we recommend caution when traveling the good shoulder.

Turn onto D18. (sign: Rouffach Nord)

Take a left at the light toward central Rouffach. We recommend a lunch stop in this quintessential cobblestoned Alsatian village, where all the views have postcard value. A very fancy *boulangerie-patisserie* is planted in the middle of the street, and cafés and restaurants are close by. One recommended vineyard is Clos St.-Landelin, whose grapes benefit from the protection of the high Vosage mountain, the Grand Ballon. You can also visit an old church and a small regional museum. Then leave town the way you entered.

Turn left on D18 bis.

You'll ride on the N83 for a few hundred feet.

Turn onto D15. (sign: Westhalten) This slightly uphill vineyard road forks left into **Soultzmatt**, where mineral springs support the town's economy and the vintage wine produced at the highest growing altitude in Alsace.

Ride through town; don't take D5.

Go right on D18 bis. (sign: Osenbach) Your route now takes you into forest at a moderate slope. The forests of Alsace are large and deep. You can well imagine Hansel and Gretel losing their way among the ancient firs, ferns, and many other varieties of flora. The feeling riding along here is more shadowed, cooler, and more mountainous than in other regions of France.

In **Osenbach,** turn right on D40. You'll see great canyons with fields on your left as you continue riding an uphill slope.

At a midforest junction, veer left on D40. (sign: Soultzbach) After a climb of several miles, pause as you near the top for incredible views of the valley out of which you've just ridden.

At the summit, go right on D40. (sign: Munster) A blissful downhill run takes you through more deep forest. The mountain air is fragrant, with a sweet, clean, deep woodsy smell. We found this to be one of the most beautiful forests in Europe.

Turn right on D2. (sign: Munster) At the bottom of 2 miles of exhilarating downhill you'll come out of the forest and into **Soultzbach**.

Turn right on D417. (sign: Colmar)

Take an *immediate* left on D2. (sign: Wihr-au-Val)

Go left onto D10. (sign: Munster) The D10 takes you through the towns of **Wihr** and **Gunsbach** into the old city of **Munster**.

WHERE TO STAY AND DINE IN MUNSTER

The two-star Hotel-Restaurant Verte Vallée is aptly named, situated in a beautiful park on the Fecht River (10 rue A.-Hartmann, 68140 Munster; tel. 89-77-15-15). The Verte Vallée could be considered a health spa, equipped as it is with a large fitness center containing a swimming pool, sauna, Turkish bath, exercise room, whirlpool, and solarium. All 107 rooms in this large, restful Swiss-looking hotel are available with television and full bathrooms. The terrace area is especially lovely. The large dining room offers an extensive menu, including duck *foie gras*, creamed sole with mushrooms, salmon in horseradish sauce, and warm cake with anise cream. You can reach the Hotel Verte Vallée by turning right on D47. (Modest)

We recommend the Verte Vallée, but there are many other hotels in the area. A less centrally located choice is Au Chene Voltaire, a small hotel 2 miles out of Munster on the D10 (route au Chene-Voltaire, at Luttenbach, 68140 Munster; tel. 89-77-31-74). This inn nestles in the middle of forest, where the modern hotel rooms are in a separate building from the more rustic restaurant. (Modest)

You may also want to consider lodging at one of the hospitable farmhouse-inns in the region, where you can experience the culture first-hand. We predict that you'll enjoy the spacious, restful feeling of this beautiful area.

SUMMARY

ALSACE TOUR: DAY ONE

Colmar to Munster

(35 miles)

- Begin in front of the train station and ride south.
- Turn right on Quartier Sud for about 200 feet.
- Go right at the next junction (sign: Equisheim).
- Ride straight across the next junction, placing you on D14 (sign: Husseren).
- Within 2½ miles you'll come to Equisheim.
- Turn left at the Husseren-les-Châteaux sign to stay on D14 for a little less than 2 miles.
- In Husseren-les-Châteaux turn onto D1 (sign: Route of the five châteaux).
- At the intersection remain on D1 (sign: Obermorschwihr).
- Cycle through Obermorschwihr and Herrlisheim-près-Colmar, a little over 2½ miles.
- Take the right on D1 XI (sign: Gueberschwihr). Keep following the signs about 3½ miles to Gueberschwihr.
- Follow the signs to Centre Ville.
- In the center of town, take the road to the left of the building that says Vins Alsace Clement Werck.
- Take the road with the Pfaffenheim sign out through vineyards. Ride less than 2 miles to Pfaffenheim.
- Turn for a short distance on the N83 (sign: Rouffach).
- Turn onto D18 (sign: Rouffach nord) for less than a mile into Rouffach.
- Take a left at the light toward central Rouffach for lunch.
- Turn left on D18 bis.
- You'll ride on the N83 for a few hundred feet.
- Turn onto D15 (sign: Westhalten) for under 3 miles to Soultzmatt.
- Ride through town; don't take D5.
- Turn right on D18 bis (sign: Osenbach) about 2½ miles into Osenbach.
- Turn right on D40.

- At a midforest junction after about 1½ miles, veer left on D40 (sign: Soultzbach).
- After 2 miles, at the summit, go right on D40 (sign: Munster)
- After 3½ miles, turn right on D2 (sign: Munster).
- After 2 miles, in Soultzbach, turn right on D417 (sign: Colmar).
- Take an *immediate* left on D2 (sign: Wihr-au-Val) for a few hundred feet.
- Go left on D10 (sign: Munster) a little over 3 miles through Wihr and Gunsbach into Munster.

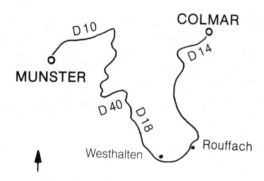

DAY TWO: MUNSTER TO RIQUEWIHR

In this 25-mile day you'll come back to the wine route via more mountain scenery and hill climbing. You'll pass through more invigorating stretches of forest, have the opportunity for a first-class lunch, then wind through your wine-tasting afternoon ride to arrive at the most-photographed and visited village in Alsace. We recommend a hearty breakfast to fuel the first challenging climb.

Leave Munster on the D417.

Turn right on D5. (sign: Hohrodberg) This section of the ride is very steep, climbing through switchbacks for a little over 6 miles. Your considerable reward is the outstanding view of the whole valley in the incredibly sweet air of the mountain village of **Hohrodberg**. There are a couple of hotels, well located for panoramic views, where you may wish to rest for a coffee break. After your stop, the road still climbs (but more moderately) through a forest of large pines.

Turn right on D11 VI. (signs: Labaroche, Trois Épis) You're still in a folklore atmosphere as the road begins to level out, emerging to overlook the valley briefly, then moving back into the moist, lush forest.

Take a right on D11. (sign: Les Trois Épis) The downhill slope carries you into **Les Trois Épis**, a popular vacation spot and our recommended lunch stop. The modest and genial Au Relais les Trois Épis is on your left. The sumptuous luxury hotel, Le Grand Hôtel (68410 Les Trois Épis; tel. 89-49-80-65), is on your right. You can dine in the Medium range in the posh dining room with delicious Alsatian lamb and beef dishes, as well as a great view. (*Note:* There is another excellent luncheon opportunity down the road in the next village, if your appetite hasn't quite ripened.)

Directly across from Le Grand Hôtel, take the D11 VIII. (sign: Ammerschwihr) You can digest your lunch as you glide downhill through more glorious forest.

Follow the sign to Ammerschwihr at the T intersection. The road now levels out and comes into vineyard territory. You come next to **Ammerschwihr**, an ancient village that was almost totally destroyed during World War II, but which has been reconstructed in the traditional manner. Some towers, a church, and the front of the Town Hall remain in their original form. Some say that Ammerschwihr has the best restaurant of the region, Aux Armes de France (tel. 89-47-10-12), whose chef, Pierre Gaertner, serves legendary and imaginative cuisine. You can dine superlatively in the Modest to Medium range from noon until 2. Wine-tasting opportunities abound.

Turn right at the first intersection.

Go left on N415. (sign: Kayserberg)

Turn right onto D10 after about 1½ miles. (sign: Kayserberg) In the famous village of **Kayserberg**, you can visit the former home of Dr. Albert Schweitzer, now a museum. The Weiss River, the Renaissance sections, and the wine-tasting all contribute to Kayserberg's popularity.

Take the D28. (sign: Ribeauville)

Stay on the D28, following the signs to Ribeauville and Sigolsheim. In **Sigolsheim**, you'll find lush vineyards covering the rolling hills.

At the roundabout, take D1 bis. (signs: Riquewihr, Ribeauville) You'll pass through a couple of villages, **Bennewihr** and **Mittelwihr**, both with wine tasting and loads of local color. Mittelwihr's unusually benign climate has given it the nickname "South of France" and a particularly delicious Riesling.

Follow the signs into Riquewihr.

WHERE TO STAY AND DINE IN RIQUEWIHR

This small, circular, walled village receives a large number of tourists during the day, but is quiet and restful at night. Be sure to book your reservations early, for the few hotels here fill rapidly. Riquewihr's structures have changed little since the sixteenth century, and there is much to see as you wander through the cobblestone streets. The wine from this area is reputedly the best in the region. Another French museum makes its home here—a museum of the history of the Alsace postal service.

Le Cerf Restaurant-Hôtel, a two-star establishment within the walled centre ville, is pleasantly provincial and full of Alsatian charm (68340 Riquewihr; tel. 89-47-92-18). The eighteen rooms are picturesque, with beamed ceilings, firm beds, and fully equipped baths. The *brasserie* serves Alsatian specialties throughout the day. (Modest)

Le Riquewihr is located within walking distance of the town and overlooks the surrounding vineyards (route de Ribeauville, 68340 Riquewihr; tel. 89-47-83-13). A more modern hotel without restaurant, its rooms have a European flavor and are quite comfortable, if somewhat utilitarian.

Restaurants abound in Riquewihr; most are accessible by walking through the walled *centre ville*. The Auberge à L'Ecurie (tel. 89-47-92-48), which has an outdoor patio, specializes in Alsatian dishes such as onion tarts and sauerkraut. We urge you to try out the locally esteemed Sarment d'Or, at the far end of the medieval section. We had salmon in a delicate lemon cream reduction, and a duck breast arrived in a hearty red wine sauce. We needed lots of strolling time to begin to recover from the several desserts and wine. It was worth it.

SUMMARY

ALSACE TOUR: DAY TWO

Munster to Riquewihr

(25 miles)

- Leave Munster on the D417.
- Turn right on D5 (sign: Hohrodberg) after about a mile.
- Climb for 4½ miles into Hohrodberg.
- Turn right on D11 VI (sign: Labaroche, Trois Épis) after 2 miles.
- Turn right on D11 (sign: Les Trois Épis) for 6 miles into Les Trois Épis and lunch.
- Directly across from Le Grand Hôtel, take the D11 VIII (sign: Ammerschwihr) approximately 9 miles into Ammerschwihr.
- Turn right at the first intersection.
- Go left on N415 (sign: Kayserberg).
- Turn right on D10 after about 1½ miles (sign: Kayserberg) and ride 2½ miles into Kayserberg.

- Take the D28 (sign: Ribeauville) less than 1 mile, following the signs to Ribeauville and into Sigolsheim.
- At the roundabout, take D1 bis (signs: Riquewihr, Ribeauville).
- You'll ride through Bennewihr and Mittlewihr on the 2½ miles into Riquewihr.

RIQUEWIHR

Kayserberg •

D 3

D 28

D 11

D 5

• Hohrodberg

MUNSTER

DAY THREE: RIQUEWIHR TO DAMBACH-LA-VILLE

This seemingly short 25-mile day takes you through more abundant vineyard country and another mountain loop, this time to the famed castle at Haut-Kœnigsbourg. For those of you more inclined to take the low road, we offer you an alternate, wine-filled route. We end the day in one of the most beautiful villages of this region and our personal favorite.

Begin the day at the roundabout in front of the old section. Go left on D3 II. (sign: Ribeauville)

Take another left onto D1 bis. (sign: Ribeauville)

We saw many cyclists in Alsace, enjoying the ride through high vineyards, where a gingerbread village is almost always on the horizon. We also saw many riders challenging themselves on the mountain roads. Riding through **Zellenberg**, you might stop for a moment to enjoy the broad view of the valley—as far as Colmar on a good day.

Follow the signs to Ribeauville. As you cruise into **Ribeauville**, you'll see a castle on the distant mountain that is one of today's treats. Ribeauville is a traditional Alsatian village with a proud heritage. Several festivals are celebrated here annually, and the half-timbered houses, shops, and museums make this a popular tourist destination. The last time we came through, Ribeauville was thronged with tourists at 10 in the morning. If you want to take a tour of this very popular town, go into the *centre ville*, then back out to the D1.

Stay on the main road, following the signs to Bergheim.

At the roundabout take the direction toward Bergheim. Bergheim still has many medieval houses and towers, as it passed through World War II relatively unscathed.

Stay on D1. You'll pass through more vineyards to **Rorschwihr** and on to **St.-Hippolyte**, whose main attraction is as the entrance road to Haut-Kœnigsbourg. This is your route choice-point. If you're in the touring, wine-tasting mood, stay in St.-Hippolyte, then continue on to Kintzheim. The next tour direction takes you on a moderately graded uphill climb for approximately 8 miles to the castle.

Just before the main part of town, turn left on D1 bis. (sign: Ht.-Kœnigsbourg) The road climbs first through vineyards, then into the spectacular Vosages mountain forests.

Turn right staying on D1 bis. (sign: Ht.-Kœnigsbourg)

Turn left on D159, which will take you all the way up to the castle. (sign: Ht.-Kœnigsbourg) As you turn onto D159, the road becomes steeper for the last part of the climb to 2,500 feet. We suggest a tour and lunch stop here in **Haut-Kœnigsbourg**, at the terrace café in front of the castle after touring, or at the Hôtel-Restaurant du Haut-Kœnigsbourg down the hill (tel. 88-92-10-92). You will feast on the view alone, stretching to the Black Forest.

The fifteenth-century castle of Haut-Kœnigsbourg is one of the most extensively and expensively restored châteaux of the country. You can join the hundreds of thousands of annual visitors in marveling at the architecture and splendid furnishings of the largest castle in Alsace.

As you leave the castle, you'll have the opportunity to turn left and circle the castle. Don't. Go straight back down the hill.

Now comes the treat of sailing downhill on the D159. (direction: Kintzheim) You'll pass a park colony of free-roaming macaques on your left as you descend through forest (sign: Montagne des Singes, which means "Monkey Mountain"). You'll emerge from the forest above Kintzheim and shortly come into town. One of the main attractions in **Kintzheim** is the extraordinary eagle training center in the castle overlooking the village. Each afternoon visitors can view controlled flights of eagles, falcons, vultures, and other birds.

Turn left on D35. (sign: Chatenois)
You are back on the Route de Vin now, riding through the small village of **Chatenois**.

At the stop light, cross to stay on D35. (sign: Scherwiller) As you come out of Chatenois, look up to the left to see the ruins of a castle. There is a turnoff here if you want to put more miles on your legs today.

Otherwise, in Scherwiller take the left on D35. (sign: Dambach) Scherwiller is one capital of Riesling production, and the beauty of its many ancient buildings is enhanced by the passage of the Aubach River.

At the roundabout follow the signs to Dambach. Pass Dieffenthal, staying on the D35 through more vineyards into **Dambach-la-Ville**.

WHERE TO STAY AND DINE IN DAMBACH

Dambach is known for its health resorts, resplendent flowers, and many beautiful buildings, labeled with fine wrought-iron signs. We enjoyed wandering through the small streets and discovered many treasures.

Two of the most appealing hotels are centrally located, and both are easily in the Modest range. The hotel-restaurant "A la Couronne" (Kientz, 13 place du Marche, 67650 Dambach-la-Ville; tel. 88-92-40-85) has comfortable rooms, many Alsatian dining selections, and very pleasant public rooms. The two-star hotel-restaurant Au Raisin d'Or (28 bis rue Clemenceau; tel. 88-92-40-08) is smaller, but equally appealing.

SUMMARY

ALSACE TOUR: DAY THREE

Riquewihr to Dambach-la-Ville

(25 miles)

- Go left on D3 II from the roundabout in front of the medieval town (sign: Ribeauville).
- Take another left shortly onto DI bis (sign: Ribeauville).
- You'll pass through Zellenberg on the almost 3 miles to Ribeauville.
- Stay on DI (after visiting), following the signs to Bergheim.
- At the roundabout take the direction toward Bergheim for 2 miles into Bergheim.
- Stay on DI 2 miles through Rorschwihr and into St.-Hippolyte.
- Just before the main part of town, turn left on DI bis (sign: Ht.-Kœnigsbourg).
- After less than a mile, turn left on DI59 (sign: Ht.-Kœnigsbourg) for a little over 3 miles to the castle and lunch.

- Go straight back down the hill.
- Take the D159 (direction: Kintzheim) for 3½ miles into Kintzheim.
- Turn left on D35 (sign: Chatenois) a little over 1 mile into Chatenois.
- Stay on D35 through Scherwiller (sign: Dambach) a little over 4 miles to Dambach.

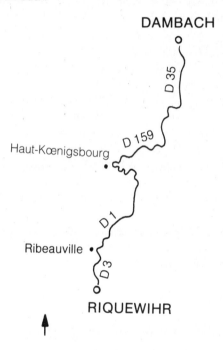

DAMBACH

D 35

D 159

Haut-Kœnigsbourg

D 1

Ribeauville

D 3

RIQUEWIHR

DAY FOUR: DAMBACH TO OBERNAI

Your mountain loop today climbs to the resting place of the patron saint of Alsace, St. Odile. The magnificent site of this former abbey is one of the highlights of this tour. The remainder of this 22-mile day is relatively level and delivers you at day's end to another prosperous, charming town.

Continue north on D35 as you leave Dambach. (sign: Bleinschweiler) This vineyard region passes through several typical wine-growing villages. **Bleinschweiler** has its main festival in July.

Stay on D35, which veers right at the intersection. (sign: Barr)

Just out of town, take a left on D35. The level road passes through **Nothalten**, then climbs slightly into **Itterswiller**.

Turn left on D35. (sign: Barr)

Take the right onto D3. (sign: Barr)

In Eichhoffen, take the left fork on D35. (sign: Barr)

Turn left on D425. (sign: Barr) In the large, distinguished town of **Barr**, you may want to stop to visit its museum of Alsatian furniture, the many ornate public buildings, and lovely homes of this "wine capital of the lower Rhine."

At the first roundabout head left. (signs: Mittelbergheim, Ste.-Odile) Several beautiful French buildings are located to your right just at the turn.

At the stop light follow the sign to Ste.-Odile.

Turn left on D854. (sign: Ste.-Odile)

At the fork just out of town, bear right. You will see a D854 sign on your left shortly. As you pass many pretty houses and grounds the road begins to climb the 6 miles to Ste.-Odile. The moderate grade leads you through forest and stone out-croppings. Stay on the main road, which bears right. You'll see another large stone marker to your left.

Take the left on D854. (sign: Ste.-Odile) You may call it "St. Ordeal" after this climb.

Turn right on D426. (sign: Ste.-Odile)

Fork right to Ste.-Odile. You've earned your lunch, available in the self-service cafeteria at the far end of the enchanting courtyard, or the small German-influenced restaurant. Ste.-Odile, the blind daughter of Duke Aldanc of Alsace, is said to have suddenly regained her sight when baptized. She founded this abbey, which was decimated by fire in the sixteenth century. The current buildings, of luminescent pink sandstone, stand on the spectacular site of many ancient cults, dating back to the sixth century B.C. Be sure to stand at the ramparts to view the valley and mountains to the south.

Take the D33 next to Ste.-Odile. (sign: Obernai) Your post-lunch downhill run provides a light and shadow stroboscopic effect as you stream through forest and field. Stop occasionally to look back up the mountain at the jutting magnificence of Ste.-Odile.

Go left on D109. (sign: Obernai) You will begin to catch glimpses of the valley now through the trees.

In the small village of St.-Nabor, go right at the Strasbourg sign.

Turn right on D109. (sign: Obernai) Continue following signs to Obernai on this tree-lined road.

At the stop sign go straight across on D109. (sign: Obernai)

Veer right at the fork. (sign: Obernai) Follow the signs on the cobblestone streets to the *centre ville* of Obernai.

WHERE TO STAY AND DINE IN OBERNAI

We have two excellent choices for your stay in this flower-bedecked and vividly authentic Alsatian town.

In the center of town you'll find Le Grand Hotel, a three-star treat with twenty-four luxurious rooms (rue Dietrich, 67210 Obernai; tel. 88-95-51-28). Mr. Bosch, owner and chef, serves French and Alsatian cuisine, including salad with duck, a five-vegetable terrine with a border of tomatoes, and steamed salmon with noodles. (Modest–Medium)

The Hotel du Parc (169 rue General-Gouraud, 67210 Obernai; tel. 88-95-50-08), aptly named by its surroundings, has fifty rooms and three different dining rooms with separate decor. The hotel is equipped with a swimming pool, sauna, solarium, and whirlpool in addition to its large, well-decorated rooms. The imaginative cuisine relies on the local fresh produce, which often includes our favorite wild mushrooms.

Obernai is one of the more interesting stops in Alsace. Be sure to visit the marketplace, the flower-bedecked place de l'Étoile, and the six-pail fountain. If you arrive in early October, you may catch the Grape Harvest Festival.

SUMMARY

ALSACE TOUR: DAY FOUR

Dambach to Obernai

(22 miles)

- Continue riding north on D35 (sign: Bleinschweiler) 1½ miles through Bleinschweiler, veering right at the intersection (sign: Barr).
- Just out of town, take a left on D35.
- Stay on D35 a little over 4 miles, through Nothalten, Itterswiller, and Eichhoffen (sign: Barr).
- Turn left on D425 (sign: Barr) for a little over 1 mile.
- At the first roundabout in Barr, head left (signs: Mittelbergheim, St.-Odile).
- At the stop light follow the sign to St.-Odile.
- Turn left on D854 (sign: St.-Odile).
- At the fork just out of town, bear right, where you'll see a D854 sign shortly.
- Follow D854 almost 5 miles.

• Turn right on D426 (sign: St.-Odile) for less than a mile, then fork right to St.-Odile and lunch.
• After lunch, take the D33 next to St.-Odile (sign: Obernai) about 3½ miles.
• Turn right on D109 (sign: Obernai) for approximately 6½ miles, following the signs into Obernai.

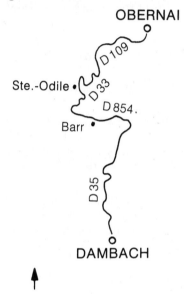

DAY FIVE: OBERNAI TO STRASBOURG

This mostly level 40-mile day carries you by the back way into our choice for Most Beautiful City in Europe: Strasbourg. You'll have your last photo opportunities in pretty wine villages and one last swing into the mountains.

Leave Obernai on the D322, near the *centre ville.* (sign: Boersch) You will shortly come into the town of **Boersch**.

At the roundabout, go into the *centre ville* **and explore, as it has often earned the** "prettiest village" **award.** Ride through the little tower into town, go around, and come back out the same way.

Turn onto D35. (sign: Rosheim)
The road rolls through cornfields here, on the way to **Rosheim.** This wine village has four medieval towers demarcating its boundaries, a twelfth-century house, and two Romanesque churches.

Go left on D435. (sign: Rosenwiller)

Turn left on D435. (sign: Rosenwiller)

Take an immediate left. (sign: Rosenwiller) Vineyards grow on the hills to the right as you climb a slight uphill grade into **Rosenwiller**, which boasts a gracious Gothic church and an ancient windmill. Climb up through town.

At the junction, turn left. (sign: Cimetière Israelite) This cemetery is the oldest Jewish burial site in Alsace, and one of the biggest. You'll climb up through forest at a slight to moderate grade.

Turn right at the junction with D604. (direction: Grendelbruch) This is your last Alsatian mountain forest. Savor the fragrant aroma and glorious air. For those of you who want to linger and challenge your legs further, continue on the forested D604 through Grendelbruch, wind around through Muhlbach, and cross the D392 to turn right on the N420 (which is surprisingly less traveled) to rejoin the tour. If you are ready to turn toward the big city, follow the directions.

Turn right on D704. (sign: Molkirch) Gather picnic supplies or eat at one of the cafés in **Molkirch**.

Continue on the D704, crossing the juncture with D392.

Turn right on N420. (sign: Heiligenberg) The N420 parallels the main thoroughfare of the D392, and passes through a series of tiny villages, some with very large names. In general, keep following the signs to Strasbourg. You'll ride through **Lutzelhouse**, **Umatt**, **Heiligenberg**, and **Dinsheim**. **Mutzig** is home to some great breweries and a military museum honoring the inventor of the rifle which ensured a French victory in 1870.

Follow the D30. (sign: Molsheim)

In **Molsheim**, take the D422 toward the *centre ville*. This large, bustling wine center has both Renaissance and Gothic churches to explore, a large fountain, and a curious town hall.

At the light, cross to stay on D422. (sign: Saverne) If you go into the *centre ville*, return to D422.

Head right at the fork. (sign: Avolsheim) We're now heading the back way into Strasbourg, a huge city where bicyclists can easily get overshadowed.

In **Avolsheim**, stay on D422.

In **Soultze-les-Bains**, turn right onto D45. (sign: Wolxheim) Vineyards appear on the hills to your left, followed by sunflower fields, corn, and more vineyards.

The road briefly turns into D30, then back into D45, which you take all the way into Strasbourg. You'll cruise through one of the biggest names in the area, **Breuschwickersheim**, and another sequence of small villages, **Achenheim**, where you'll notice a bike path on the left, **Oberschaeffolsheim**, and **Wolfisheim**.

Now you will start hitting the lights and residential areas of Strasbourg's suburbs. After days in the less-trafficked areas of Alsace, use caution in heavy rushing traffic.

You'll join the N4.

Follow the signs to Centre Ville. You'll ride under the A35.

Turn right at the sign to the cathedral.

Take a left at the Centre Ville sign. Continue following the signs to Cathédrale and Centre Ville, which will lead you over bridges into the old city of **Strasbourg**.

WHERE TO STAY AND DINE IN STRASBOURG

Strasbourg has many hotels in every price range and with endless combinations of desired features. One possibility is to pick up the Hotel and Restaurant Guide at one of the offices of tourism and call to find the most suitable accommodations. We recommend staying at least one extra night to have time to explore this exceptionally beautiful city—Paris without the smog and congestion.

We suggest a splurge at the four-star Sofitel Strasbourg (place St.-Pierre-le-Jeune; tel. 88-32-99-30), located in the city center, adjacent to one of the city's oldest churches. This hotel will pamper you with soundproofing (so welcome in any large city), full luxury amenities, and a light and cheerful ambiance. As in most of Strasbourg, the cuisine is international. (Top)

The Terminus-Gruber offers more traditional French decor and hospitality behind its somewhat forbidding exterior (10 place de la Gare; tel. 88-32-87-00). One highlight of this hotel is its impeccable and luxurious bathrooms, a feature we grew extremely fond of after long days in the saddle. The three-star Terminus-Gruber has two restaurants and a *brasserie* from which to choose. (Middle–Top)

We had the most fun dining (or snacking, we should say) by strolling through the old city and sampling the wares at various booths, cafés, and open-air markets. Alsatians seem to be extremely fond of ice cream. Your hotel and restaurant guide offers many suggestions for fancier cuisine.

Also available at the office of tourism, and very useful, is the *Plan de Strasbourg*, a tourist map in three languages. Use it to help navigate your way to the interesting sights of

Strasbourg. The most prominent and magnificent attraction is the cathedral, a stunning sight that dominates the old city. View it at different times of day, especially late afternoon, to appreciate the play of light on the intricate facade. Strasbourg has a thriving café and street scene, best observed from an outdoor café in the place Kleber. You'll see aging hippies and many ethnic groups mingling among the street wares and hear the happy hum of commerce. Many people like to view the city from the comfortable seats of a river cruise, which will take you along the canals surrounding the old city in about an hour. Strasbourg houses a fine eighteenth-century château, a fascinating museum of medieval and Renaissance art and many other artifacts from the region, and many gorgeous houses in La Petite France section. Park your bikes and take a walking tour the best to admire this brilliant jewel.

SUMMARY

ALSACE TOUR: DAY FIVE

Obernai to Strasbourg

(40 miles)

- Depart from Obernai on the D322, near the *centre ville* (sign: Boersch).
- After 2½ miles, in Boersch, turn onto D35 (sign: Rosheim) and ride for almost 2 miles into Rosheim.
- Go left on D435 (sign: Rosenwiller), and turn left to stay on D435.
- Take an immediate left (sign: Rosenwiller) for less than 2 miles into Rosenwiller.
- At the junction, turn left (sign: Cimetière Israelite) for a little over a mile.
- Turn right at the junction with D604 (sign: Grendelbruch) and cycle for about 2 miles.
- Turn right on D704 (sign: Molkirch). Continue on D704 through Molkirch for 3½ miles.
- Turn right on N420 (sign: Heiligenberg) and keep following the signs to Strasbourg.

- You'll pass through the villages of Lutzelhouse, Umatt, Heiligenberg, and Dinsheim in these almost 8 miles.
- In Mutzig follow D30 (sign: Molsheim) for about 1½ miles into Molsheim.
- Take the D422 toward the *centre ville.*
- At the light, cross to stay on D422 (sign: Saverne).
- Head right at the fork (sign: Avolsheim). Strasbourg is about 11 miles through suburbs from here.
- In Avolsheim stay on D422.
- In Soultze-les-Bains, turn right onto D45 (sign: Wolxheim). The road briefly turns into D30, then back into D45, which you take all the way into Strasbourg. You'll pass through Breuschwickersheim, Achenheim, Oberschaeffolsheim, and Wolfisheim.
- You'll join the N4.
- Follow the signs to Centre Ville, riding under the A35.
- Turn right at the sign to the cathedral.
- Take a left at the Centre Ville sign, coming into Strasbourg.

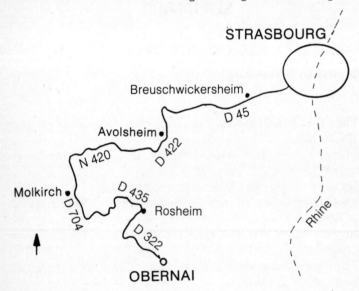

APPENDIX ONE:

SELECTED TOUR

COMPANIES OFFERING

CYCLING TRIPS

THROUGH FRANCE

HERE IS A SELECTION OF TOURING COMPANIES OFFERING trips through some of the same territory we describe. Since an organized tour represents a sizeable investment of your time and money, it is wise to put a commensurate amount of energy into selecting the company with whom you want to travel. Brochures can be helpful, but we recommend calling the office to talk personally with representatives of the company. Most will be happy to talk to you, and even to put you in touch with tour leaders. *Bon voyage!*

Backcountry Bicycle Tours, P.O. Box 4029, Bozeman, MT 59772; (406) 586-3556

Bike Quest, P.O. Box 332, Brookdale, CA 95007; (408) 338-2477

Bike Tour France, P.O. Box 32814, Charlotte, NC 28232; (704) 527-0955

Butterfield and Robinson, 70 Bond Street, Toronto, Ontario, M5B 1X3, Canada; (800) 387-1147

Chateaux Bike Tours (Formerly Bicycle France, Ltd.), P.O. Box 276, Denver, CO 80201; (303) 296-6972

Country Cycling Tours, 140 W. 83rd St., New York, NY 10024; (212) 874-5151

Euro-Bike Tours, P.O. Box 40, DeKalb, IL 60115; (815) 758-8851

Europeds, 883 Sinex Ave., Pacific Grove, CA 93950; (408) 372-1173

Gerhard's Bicycle Oddyseys, 4949 S.W. Macadam Ave., Portland, OR 97201; (503) 223-2402

International Bicycle Touring Society, P.O. Box 6979, San Diego, CA 92106; (619) 226-TOUR (8687)

Progressive Travels, Ltd., P.O. Box 775164, Steamboat Springs, CO 80477; (800) 245-2229

(For Children) Riding High Bicycle Tours for Kids, P.O. Box 14848, Portland, OR 97214; (503) 293-2143

Ten-Speed Tours, P.O. Box 7152, Van Nuys, CA 91409; (818) 786-4279

Ultimate Country Cycling Tours, 30 Cedar Ave., Pointe Claire, Quebec H9S 4Y1, Canada; (514) 697-9496

Vermont Country Cyclers, P.O. Box 145 Bas, Waterbury Center, VT (802) 244-5215

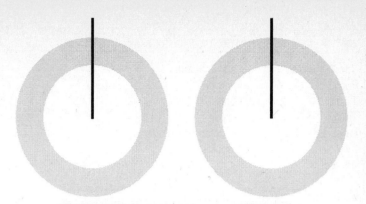

APPENDIX TWO:
USEFUL FRENCH
BICYCLING WORDS

YOUR PORTABLE FRENCH DICTIONARY PROBABLY WILL not have many of the following obscure bicycle terms. For simplicity's sake, we will start toward the front of a bicycle and work toward the back.

Bicycle	*vélo* (commonly used term), *bicyclette* (not as widely used)
Handlebars	*guidon*
Upright handlebars	*guidon de droit*
Brake lever	*poignées*
Light	*lumière*
Brakes	*freins*
Gear shift lever	*manette de changement de vitesses*
Quick-release hub	*blockage rapide*
Cable	*cable*
Headset	*jeu de direction*
Front fork	*fourche avant*
Water bottle	*réserve d'eau*

Bottle holder	*porte bidon*
Pump	*pompe*
Tire	*pneu*
Spoke	*rayon*
Inner tube	*la chambre d'aire*
Rim	*jante de roue*
Valves	*à la française* (Presta type), *à l'anglaise* (Schrader)
Valve cap	*capuchon*
Crank	*manivelles*
Bottom bracket	*boite de pedalier*
Pedal	*pedales*
Toe clip	*cale-pied*
Strap for toe clip	*courroie de cale-pied*
Chain	*chaine*
Saddle	*selle*
Seat tube	*tige de selle*
Derailleur	*derailleur*
Back sprocket	*pignons*
Hub	*moyeu*
Rack	*porte baggage*

BICYCLE TOURS OF ITALY

by Gay and Kathlyn Hendricks

Savor the rich sights, sounds, and flavors of Italy while enjoying America's fastest growing new sport—bicycle touring. Thousands of adventurous Americans have already traded in the rigors of high-stress, high-cost travel for the fun of biking it to the world's greatest getaways. And now you can do it, too. With this extraordinary guide, you'll learn everything you need to know to put your vacation plans in gear.

There's an epidemic with 27 million victims. And no visible symptoms.

It's an epidemic of people who can't read.

Believe it *or* not, 27 million Americans are functionally illiterate, about one adult in five.

The solution to this problem is you... when you join the fight against illiteracy. So call the Coalition for Literacy at toll-free **1-800-228-8813** and volunteer.

Volunteer Against Illiteracy. The only degree you need is a degree of caring.